EVALUATION SOURCEBOOK

For Private and Voluntary Organizations

BLANCHE CASE
Consortium for Community Self
Help/United Israel Appeal

ELAINE EDGCOMB
Consultant

MERRILL EWERT
MAP International

DAVID HERRELL
Christian Children's Fund

PATRICIA HUNT
American Friends Service
Committee

SUZANNE KINDERVATTER
Overseas Education Fund

JEANNE McCORMACK
World Education

DONALD MILLER
Compassion International

RICHARD REDDER
Meals for Millions/Freedom from
Hunger Foundation

RAY RIGNALL
CARE

JIM RUGH
World Neighbors

ARMIN SCHMIDT
Heifer Project International

JOSEPH SPRUNGER
Lutheran World Relief

PETER VAN BRUNT
Save the Children

DAO SPENCER
American Council of Voluntary Agencies for Foreign Service

edited by
Daniel Santo Pietro
Project Coordinator

A publication of the American Council of Voluntary Agencies for Foreign Service through the
"Approaches to Evaluation" project

NEW YORK

Library of Congress Card Catalog Number 83-071468

ISBN 0-932140-01-7

Published 1983 by the American Council of Voluntary Agencies for Foreign Service, Inc.

"Approaches to Evaluation"
ACVAFS
200 Park Avenue South
New York, N.Y. 10003

TABLE OF CONTENTS

ACKNOWLEDGEMENTS

The idea of a sourcebook came from the original planners of the "Approaches to Evaluation" project. They recognized a gap in evaluation literature as an obstacle to PVO practitioners. None of us at the beginning of the project could foresee the precise content of the *Sourcebook*. Needless to say, it has been a fascinating process watching it take form from the contributions of so many people. There is no master sculptor of this work, but many skilled craftspersons to thank.

In first place comes the work of the Task Force. They represent a cross-section of private and voluntary organizations (PVOs) from all parts of the country. Their collective experience and commitment to evaluation is outstanding. Each member unselfishly gave time to design, discuss and critique the draft of this *Sourcebook*. Although it is difficult to identify one person as the author of any section, certain Task Force members did make particular contributions. Merrill Ewert and I are primarily responsible for Section I. Jeanne McCormack provided the thread for "Thinking Through an Evaluation Strategy". Elaine Edgcomb did most of the research and preparation of "The Primary Persuasions." Suzanne Kindervatter coordinated and drafted much of the chapter on "Useful Tools." Don Miller drafted "Some Thoughts on Evaluation Utilization." Lastly, I take responsibility for editing and the final organization of the *Sourcebook*'s contents. Throughout the *Sourcebook*, I have tried to be clear in attributing to numerous individuals and agencies their particular contributions.

There are numerous other persons in the PVO community who contributed in many ways to the development of the *Sourcebook*. I want to acknowledge specifically Ricardo Puerta and Jim Noel, both then with PACT, and Jairo Arboleda from Save the Children for their advice and participation in our workshops. Jairo most ably moderated the last two workshops. Of course, all those who participated in our workshops deserve a portion of the credit for getting us to this point.

Another group of individuals we need to thank are all the resource people who participated in our workshops. Our greatest success was to find challenging people who shared our interests and brought us new insights. Several of them are cited in the text. They are:

Mary Anderson — an economist with extensive experience in both the PVO and academic world. Presently an independent consultant, she was a major presenter in our Wingspread Conference and at a follow-up session on evaluation and policy.

Robert T. Bruce — Professor of Cooperative Extension, Department of Continuing Education, Cornell University. Author of various works on evaluation, he provided his practical insights in the two workshops on monitoring and impact evaluation.

Philip Coombs — Vice Chairman of the International Council for Educational Development. He is the editor of *Meeting the Basic Needs of the Rural Poor*. He spoke in our workshop on impact evaluation.

Richard R. Johnson — Research Director, Exxon Education Foundation. He has acted as an adviser throughout the project. He participated in the Wingspread Conference.

Sara M. Steele — Professor of Cooperative Extension in the Department of Continuing and Vocational Education, University of Wisconsin-Madison. She has written extensively on her practical experience with evaluation. Besides participating in the Wingspread Conference, she critiqued draft portions of the Sourcebook.

A final group to acknowledge are the donors. Their foresight made our work possible. All the PVOs who participated merit our thanks for their support of this community effort. These agencies bore about two-thirds of the cost of the project. Twelve agencies particularly deserve our appreciation for their grants to the project. They are: CARE, Catholic Relief Services, Christian Children's Fund, Church World Service, Foster Parents Plan International, Heifer Project International, Lutheran World Relief, Meals for Millions/Freedom from Hunger Foundation, PACT, Save the Children, United Israel Appeal and World Relief Corporation. The project's success is directly attributable to their generous cooperative spirit. The Office of Private and Voluntary Cooperation of the Agency for International Development funded the other third of project costs. This public-private dimension of the funding enhances the significance of the project. Our grant officer, Ross Edgar Bigelow, deserves special thanks for the effectiveness of this cooperation.

The Johnson Foundation made a special contribution by hosting our conference on evaluation and policy at Wingspread, their meeting center in Racine, Wisconsin. Their hospitality and efficiency will be long remembered.

This cooperative venture involved many unselfish people. The American Council of Voluntary Agencies for Foreign Service and the Technical Assistance Information Clearing House staff consistently lent assistance when asked. I particularly want to thank Dao N. Spencer for her guidance and support. Finally, the production of the *Sourcebook* taxed everyone's ingenuity. Fran Cohn patiently worked on the many drafts of the manuscript. David Rosen copyedited the text with remarkable skill. Suzanne Hackett designed the book with consummate care. My sincere gratitude goes to everyone associated with the project.

Daniel Santo Pietro
Project Coordinator

New York
March, 1983

FOREWORD

The principal purpose of the ACVAFS is to insure maximum effective use of the American public's contributions to its members' programs through consultation, coordination and joint planning. In keeping with this goal, over the years it has encouraged the voluntary agencies to strengthen their program management and evaluation skills. A limited review of the state of the art in evaluation among its member agencies was carried out through a series of workshops between December 1976 and October 1977.

The current "Approaches to Evaluation" project is the continuation of that effort but involving the broader private and voluntary community. The project was proposed at a 1979 conference of the Agency for International Development with private voluntary organizations. It received impetus from the PVO community which desired, however, to keep so sensitive a topic as evaluation a private initiative. Together with two consortia, CODEL and PACT, the American Council responded to a request "to provide a community-wide forum on evaluation," and created the opportunity for all interested private and voluntary agencies to participate in the project. The community's enthusiastic response took many forms: through staff participation in the preparation of the statement "Evaluation in the PVO Community," in the formulation of workshop agendas, the sharing of experience and case-studies, writing sections of this *Sourcebook* and providing generous financial and in-kind contributions.

As the major donor to many private and voluntary organizations, the Agency for International Development had a special interest in the project. While remaining sensitive to the agencies' expressed desire to keep the project under private auspices, they provided important support to complement PVO contributions.

The *Sourcebook* represents the culmination of a three-year long and truly cooperative undertaking of the private and voluntary agencies. It also represents a fine example of genuine partnership between the public and private sectors in an important area of common interest, that of evaluation. Since the beginning of the Project all efforts were made to avoid using highly technical language and to produce a document easily readable by program implementers in the field as well as by donors in developed countries.

The foundations of the project were laid down by the Ad Hoc Committee on Evaluation whose chairmen, Edgar Stoesz and Charles Fluegel, although no longer active in the project, deserve special thanks for their leadership. The ACVAFS Executive Committee and its Executive Director, Leon O. Marion, have generously made available staff time and facilities in support of the project. The project coordinator, Daniel Santo Pietro, has single-mindedly performed the nearly impossible task of putting together three major workshops, numerous subsessions and meetings, and the contents of this *Sourcebook* during the past two years.

It is our hope that users of the *Sourcebook* will find it a practical guide for selecting appropriate tools for field-based program evaluation. It is also the project planners' hope that the *Sourcebook* will serve as a catalyst for wide participation in the evaluation process as a component of good program management, rather than as a one-time undertaking.

As the *Sourcebook* is used in future training sessions and in other settings, we hope to be able to refine it to reflect new experiences. With this constant improvement in mind we will welcome comments from concerned and thoughtful users.

Dao N. Spencer,
Assistant Executive Director, ACVAFS
Approaches to Evaluation Project Administrator

EVALUATION SOURCEBOOK

For Private and Voluntary Organizations

INTRODUCTION: HOW TO USE THIS SOURCEBOOK

First, Approach this book with a spirit of inquiry. Its goal is to offer other PVO practitioners the benefit of relevant experience and insights. Foremost in our minds is to engage our colleagues in a search for answers to difficult questions we all must deal with. This *Sourcebook* is clearly an unfinished work and each reader joins the task.

Second, Read these pages as you would a guidebook. One glance should convince the reader to absorb the information in stages. Section I is important because it describes where we are coming from and trying to go. Section II introduces the Evaluation Clock which provides a framework of twelve questions for implementing evaluation. The clock symbol appears throughout this section to guide you to material pertaining to specific questions. You can use many parts (e.g., charts, chapters and PVO experiences) independently to help you conduct evaluation or enrich your agency discussions. Finally, Section III offers many practical ways to bolster your own knowledge. To help you use our working bibliography, some sources cited in the text are followed by a reference number, e.g. (Ref. 1). This reference indicates more information on this source is available in the corresponding category of the bibliography.

Third, Carry the *Sourcebook* with you on field trips. You may find opportunities to share parts with colleagues and test some of the ideas on the spot. The PVO Experiences should particularly prove useful. We are looking forward to enriching this work through reactions, particularly from the people we work with in the Third World.

Fourth, Use the *Sourcebook* in training opportunities. We see this information as a contribution to filling a gap in evaluation literature. The Sourcebook will serve as a primary resource for future workshops of the "Approaches to Evaluation" Project. We are planning a supplementary training packet building on it. Naturally, we are most interested in cooperating with PVOs in this area.

Above all, Think evaluatively as you read. The PVOs involved in this project are committed to the development of people throughout the world. If this *Sourcebook* helps even a bit to make their task more effective, it is well worth the effort.

WELCOME TO EVALUATION

CHAPTER ONE

THE EVALUATION CONTEXT

An evaluation sourcebook is important for the PVO community at this time. This Sourcebook represents a critical stage in the examination of our own practices. It represents an effort to develop evaluation approaches that are suitable for differing PVO programming styles and, most critically, for the people we are trying to serve in the Third World.

Why the Concern about Evaluation Now?
Evaluation has become increasingly important to us because, since the 1970's, there have been tremendous changes in PVO programming. There has been greater emphasis on development goals, on integrated programs, and on increasing participant involvement and control over these activities. These changes have raised new questions about our effectiveness — what works and what doesn't, and what we are best suited to do.

The changes of the 1970's made us, on the one hand, important vehicles for participatory programs and innovative community development activities. On the other hand, we have come to rely more upon government grants and other large donor support. These changes brought with them not only a legitimate requirement of accountability, but also increased pressure to use evaluation. Unfortunately, not all evaluation approaches have been amenable to our programs. Our desire to learn from experience has been frustrated by confusion over the subject of evaluation.

The tasks facing PVOs today have been compounded by a shrinking resource base. This situation has stimulated executives and program staffs to view evaluation as an aid in making difficult decisions regarding program priorities, countries of operation, and project approaches. Evaluation can help us to form policy and to answer program questions at the field level.

There is a pressing need for the PVO community to learn more about the process of evaluation. We have had to go beyond the experimental, quantitatively-oriented designs which have long been the hallmarks of evaluation. Unfortunately, we have found little evaluation literature that speaks directly to our situation — to our need to develop low-cost, small-scale, highly participatory, internally-organized approaches. We have sought to develop new approaches by learning from each other's experience, and we have called upon the resources of the community for solutions to many of the particular problems we have faced.

The Approaches to Evaluation Project
The Approaches to Evaluation Project was conceived at a 1979 AID/PVO conference. The American Council of Voluntary Agencies for Foreign Service (ACVAFS) together with two PVO consortiums, PACT and CODEL, formed the Ad Hoc Subcommittee on Evaluation to "organize and maintain a community-wide forum on evaluation and to establish priorities, evaluation topics and activities that are of primary interest and concern to the PVO community." The Ad Hoc Subcommittee, with six agency representatives, organized its work in three parts: (1) drafting a paper setting a framework in which to consider the various types of evaluation and the principle issues the agencies faced; (2) administering a questionnaire to 122 PVOs regarding their needs in program and project evaluation; and (3) developing recommendations to the directors of ACVAFS, PACT and CODEL for the creation of a project to satisfy PVO needs. This position paper, "Evaluation in the PVO Community," was widely circulated in the community. The recommendations were reviewed and approved by ACVAFS' Development Assistance Committee and Executive Committee. The project was initiated with the creation of a nine-member steering committee.

The project had three components:
1. A series of workshops for PVO executive and program staff on monitoring, impact and policy evaluation, and their relationship to larger development issues,

2. The preparation of a resource manual to include workshop findings, PVO experiences, and additional reference material useful to the PVO constituency,

3. A follow-up consultation service for agencies requesting aid on specific evaluation problems.

These components are aimed at more effectively integrating evaluation into the programming cycle and, consequently, increasing our ability to serve low-income groups in the Third World.

What Has Happened?
The project has held three workshops that have brought together 91 PVO representatives from 50 agencies representing diverse segments of the community. These workshops — Monitoring, May, 1981; Impact,

Exhibit I-A

Definitions of Monitoring and Impact Evaluation prepared by PVO Practitioners as part of synthesis papers for workshops — 1981

MONITORING is defined as a systematic process, which occurs within the context of a program or project implementation, and which has as its aim the provision of information on progress. That information has several intended uses:
1. to assist decision-making, especially in the short term, for increased project effectiveness,
2. to ensure accountability to all levels within the project hierarchy — from local community to donor — especially in financial matters,
3. to enable judgements to be made on personal and institutional performances.

The potential users of the information generated include the PVO (both the on-site project team and the headquarters based management), the community groups directly participating in the project, indigenous PVOs involved in project implementation, and the external donors. With this number of interested parties and the differing priorities which each places on the purposes for monitoring, it is easy to see how the process can be strongly tension-provoking. Its role in supervision and oversight can often inhibit the creation of an atmosphere conducive to open examination and correction. Nevertheless, in ideal circumstances, the several levels of review and purpose can mesh into a continuum in which all parties' needs are served, and it is this ideal which should be the aim in PVO projects despite the difficulties inherent in the effort.

—*Impact Evaluation Workshop Report*,
p. 33. (REF. 1)

IMPACT EVALUATION is, first and foremost, a tool for learning and an integral part of the program management process. To that end, it should be undertaken systematically, at the level of an agency's general capability, and serve as an essential element in decision making.

It involves a judgement on the project by the participants and by the PVO itself which addresses not only the accomplishment of project objectives, but other questions which are often more important than whether the project's purpose has been achieved or not. These include:
1. an understanding of the social, economic and political context in which the project takes place and whether the objectives and project design make sense in terms of this reality,
2. an analysis of the unplanned results as well as the planned ones, and
3. an assessment of the more qualitative, social process occurring with the assistance of project support.

Unlike monitoring, which is a system to provide regular information for improved project effectiveness, impact evaluation is undertaken on a longer-term, more periodic basis, and seeks to determine the ultimate value of the agency endeavor in terms of the participants' viewpoint and achievements.

—*Wingspread Conference Report*, p. 9. (REF. 1)

October, 1981; and Policy Making and Evaluation [Wingspread Conference], March, 1982 — have engaged executive and program staff in a collaborative approach. Using outside consultants, the workshops emphasized documentation of current experience and joint problem-solving, as well as provided an opportunity for reflection on the state of the art. Between workshops, core groups of participants met to explore topics of special concern, such as participation and better mechanisms for exchanging information.

At the conclusion of the workshop series, a task force was set up that included five PVO practitioners all experienced in evaluation and a majority of steering committee members. The task force met in May 1982, and planned this Sourcebook. They met again in October and reviewed their initial draft. This book is a result of their collaborative effort.

From this experience we have derived a greater awareness of ourselves as a community. We have developed a shared framework for evaluation, reached consensus on its definition for PVOs, determined what monitoring and impact evaluation mean to us.

We have come to see the value of participation in the evaluation process. Participation is important not only from the groups and communities we assist, but also at all levels within our agencies. This approach was further affirmed by the Executive Directors at the policy workshop at Wingspread.

The Sourcebook, then, is directed first and foremost at PVO practitioners in the field and in headquarters. We hope it stimulates creativity in the planning and implementing of evaluations, both by them and by their indigenous collaborating agencies. The Sourcebook is also designed for PVO executives and policy-makers who need to coordinate and utilize evaluations.

The rest of this Section further defines the nature of evaluation. It develops the rationale and the principles we consider essential for evaluation in the PVO community.

CHAPTER TWO

WHAT IS EVALUATION

In this chapter, we will describe our understanding of evaluation, drawing principally on the workshop discussions.

The Mystique of Evaluation
Misconceptions about evaluations are the greatest obstacles to conducting them. At the start of the project, our position paper proposed a definition of evaluation accepted by most PVOs.

Evaluation is
  an integral part of the management of development projects designed to:
  1. identify, during the life of a project, its strengths, weaknesses and relevance to local conditions,

  2. assess the impact of a project on the lives of local community members,

  3. analyze the results and apply the lessons learned to project and program planning, PVO policies and development strategies.

  quote from *Evaluation in the PVO Community*, ACVAFS, 1979, p. 1

Our workshop series confronted the task of shaping these general propositions into a framework for doing evaluation. Time and again, the workshops had to vanquish misconceptions like the following about the mystique of evaluation: "Evaluation requires a complex research approach that is beyond our capabilities," "You need qualified specialists to produce acceptable evaluations," "Evaluation is something AID does for us anyway." These laments came up frequently. Our most important accomplishment in the workshops was recognition that PVO PRACTITIONERS CAN DO QUALITY EVALUATION!

> Dispel the mystique of evaluation, and the myth that only an "evaluation specialist" can do it. It can be done by any analytically minded person with good practical experience and a broad, objective outlook. There are many such people in voluntary organizations. This is not to say that experienced evaluation experts cannot be helpful, particularly at the design stage and in reviewing the findings. But look out for the type that engages in "methodological overkill", and whose approach is so narrow and quantitive that it gives a very incomplete and lopsided picture.
>
> Philip Coombs, *Impact Evaluation Workshop Report*, p. 5. (REF. 1)

Recent History of Evaluation

Let us examine briefly the recent history of evaluation. The concept of using scientific evaluation to assess the impact of social programs began with the New Deal when the government for the first time invested massive sums to reach specific social objectives. Evaluation research, in the 1950's and 1960's, was the domain of the social scientist, who used it in the search for solutions to social problems. The research in this era led to some remarkable discoveries, such as the effectiveness of the Head Start program.

As studies become more sophisticated, a preoccupation with their effectiveness emerged. This is understandable. After all, the U.S. Government's rationale for spending up to $1 billion dollars annually for program evaluation is the need to make decisions that affect much larger sums. Most evaluations strictly followed a scientific method dependent on deductive analysis within a controlled design using quantitative data. Although social scientists such as Carol Weiss and Peter Rossi strived to adapt this methodology more to social action programs in the 1970's, concern grew over its usefulness. Particularly in recent years, there has been recognition among evaluation specialists that the field needs to broaden its approach by using more inductive, qualitative methods. A recent book by Michael Patton, *Qualitative Evaluation Methods*, suggests "a paradigm of choices" that encourages gathering evidence using different standards of validity than those traditionally employed.

Exhibit I-B
Attributes of Quantitative and Qualitative Paradigms

Qualitative	Quantitative
"Concerned with *understanding* human behavior from the actor's own frame reference"	"Seeks the *facts* or *causes* of social phenomena with little regard for the subjective states of individuals"
Naturalistic and controlled observation	Obtrusive and controlled measurement
Subjective	Objective
Close to the data, the "insider" perspectives	Removed from the data; the "outsider" perspective
Process-oriented	Outcome-oriented
Valid: "rich" data	Reliable "hard" data
Assumes a dynamic reality	Assumes a stable reality

The "Paradigm of Choices"

The significance of this debate among social scientists should not be lost on PVOs. Our conceptions of evaluation frequently reflect the old emphasis on controlled research and design and on quantitative data. Introduced to most PVOs in the 1970's, the logical framework, although a useful analytic tool, perpetuates this bias. Many PVO practitioners remain in a quandry. That is not difficult to understand. There are contrasting attributes to both qualitative and quantitative approaches. As Sara Steele pointed out in our last workshop, "to have meaning, methods and activities need to be grounded in and relate harmoniously to the general perspectives that we hold." PVOs should view the broadening perspective of evaluation as a creative opportunity to forge an evaluation approach that is both harmonious to our perspective and scientifically valid.

The Value Premise of Evaluation

Because PVO value systems permeate the programs they implement, we have recognized in our discussions the importance of having evaluations also reflect these values. We want to be scientific but not detached, valid in our findings but always fixed in the framework that people are authors of their own development.

A PVO EXPERIENCE

Looking back at our attempts to create participatory evaluation mechanisms for these projects, there are some important lessons to be learned.

Program policy is more than something which is made, refined, changed or abandoned. Within program policy are the values and norms, the ideologies, purposes and beliefs of an organization. Embedded in policies are the defining belief systems of organizations.

Mary Anderson
Presenter

[Evaluation] has to speak to the whole question of the reassurance of agency belief systems. . . . It has to speak to the mythology of what the agency says it has been, is going to be, what it serves, how it does, and so on. It can't disregard it. It can't destroy the identity balloon of the agency.

James MacCracken
Executive Director, Christian Children's Fund
Transcribed from Wingspread Conference

Private voluntary organizations have historically played a central role in providing social services in the Third World. Although developed differently, and for a variety of purposes, PVOs share several characteristics. First, they are formed on the basis of a common interest.

Second, membership or participation is voluntary. Third, they are, by definition, independent of the state.

The common interests shared by those involved in a private voluntary organization reflect the basic value structure of that organization. The projection of one particular goal or the organization of a certain set of activities indicates what program administrators perceive as consistent with the basic value system of their organization. Similarly, the interpretations assigned to the basic facts regarding the activities of PVOs reflect the values of those involved.

Value Premise of Organizations

Although private voluntary organizations differ greatly in terms of the purposes for which they were established and the activities through which those purposes are achieved, PVOs working in the field of development hold several values in common:

1. *People are responsible for their own development.*
   Change is not something to be imposed by external change agents from the outside, but by the prerogative of those who live in the community and share the risks involved in the decision-making process. That people should determine their own development agendas and make decisions regarding programs which affect them is the most basic value held by most voluntary agencies.

2. *Change is possible.* The optimistic view of humankind which suggests that change is possible is a second value held by PVO's. Change occurs as people examine their own problems and identify solutions that involve learning new knowledge and related skills, which, in turn, are translated into appropriate behaviors that improve the quality of life.

3. *Change occurs in community.* Although people make some decisions in isolation and take action as individuals, effective change is most likely to occur if it is community-based. The diagnosis of the problem is likely to be most accurate, the solutions proposed most appropriate, and the support for the process most pervasive where decisions regarding the local development agenda are made by individuals in the community.

4. *Development is growth.* Lasting development is that process through which people grow in their ability to take control over their own lives and improve the conditions of life which affect them. The most meaningful changes are those that occur within people themselves and which reflect an increased capacity for initiating and carrying out social change.

5. *Development workers are enablers.* Given the above values, the

task of the development worker is to enable people to effect changes in their own lives and communities. This assumes that the purpose of development activity is not to generate measurable changes according to some socio-economic indicators, but to enhance the skills of people in identifying problems, and proposing and implementing appropriate solutions.

These values profoundly affect the way the results of development activity are evaluated. A belief that people are responsible for their own development implies that the ability of outside agencies to generate social change is very limited. The appropriate indicator of a successful program endorsing this value may be the extent to which people have been able to identify their own problems, rather than whether or not a particular activity had the predicted effect on some behavior targeted for change in an organization's planning document.

The belief that change is possible and that change best occurs in community places a greater emphasis on the process by which change occurs rather than on the results of change. The indicator of success is, therefore, the extent to which people in a community are able to identify a problem, and form a concensus to propose appropriate mechanisms to address that problem. The underlying definition of change as growth in human capacity is more concerned with increasing the ability for autonomous control of decisions than with changes that can be statistically measured. Similarly, recognizing development workers as enablers means that their relative success or failure should be determined by the increasing ability of people to progressively take greater control over their own lives.

To define the meaning of evaluation for PVOs, we have looked at evaluation in broad scope and at our own special needs. We must now find a system of evaluation that will achieve the harmony we seek.

CHAPTER THREE

PUTTING EVALUATION INTO ACTION

In our workshop discussions, three broad principles emerged as essential elements for effective evaluations by PVOs. The key words are "Participatory", "Systematic" and "Simple Methodologies."

The Participatory Approach

PARTICIPATION warrants special attention among PVOs for two reasons. One focuses on its practicality. Projects will be more effective if community members are actively involved in all phases. The other stresses that participation is what development is about: gaining skills for self-reliance. In our first workshop, participants stressed that evaluation must be viewed as a dialogue. Information comes out of and is fed into a community process directed toward action.

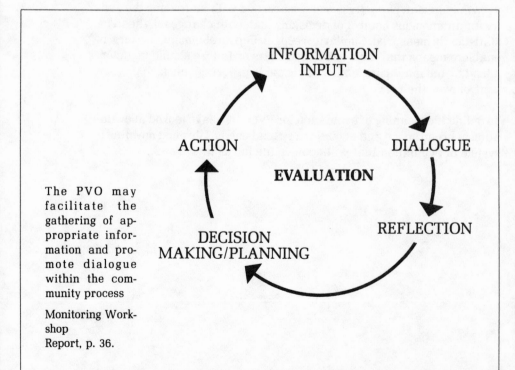

INFORMATION INPUT

ACTION

EVALUATION

DIALOGUE

DECISION MAKING/PLANNING

REFLECTION

The PVO may facilitate the gathering of appropriate information and promote dialogue within the community process

Monitoring Workshop Report, p. 36.

Participation is also important within a PVO. Consistent with community involvement in evaluation and decision-making is the involvement of staff at all levels in a similar process within the agency.

In our discussions, many felt that the concept of participation in evaluation should be extended to include donors. This can create difficulties, because of the time needed to collect and analyze evidence. But involving donors in the process may alleviate misunderstandings and make them more aware of the advantages of participation.

A Systematic Flow of Information
In our Wingspread Conference, Sara Steele cautioned against "the trap of an evaluation" as a formal project, undertaken sporadically, often by contracted outside evaluators. Our point of view is that every agency should employ all practical means to gather evidence, both quantitative and qualitative, about the impact of its programs. It should be considered the responsibility of all staff involved with programming. Evaluation should be integrated into the management cycle of programming, which includes budgeting and policy decision making.

Like most modern organizations, PVOs often suffer from information glut. At the same time, demands for evaluative information come from several different audiences, including the community, host government agencies, PVO field offices, headquarter staff and governing boards. Although the common tendency is to inundate each user with information, in the end this blunts the effect of evaluation.

In our discussions, we uncovered two remedies. One emphasized a selectivity in determining what to evaluate. The other focused on distinguishing the kind of information needed by various audiences. PVOs evaluate at different levels. The basic level is usually the project. On the next level, projects are often clustered in country programs or in some cases sectorally. The agency's overall impact in terms of its strategic goals represents yet another level. A system of evaluation must recognize that although each project ideally has its own evaluation process, the amount of information passed on from level to level should be restricted. The object is to create a steady flow of information essential for making decisions without overloading the system.

Simple But Pervasive Methodologies
Once we dispel the mystique of evaluation, only our creativity limits us. Instead of the image of the detached experimental scientist collecting data, the PVO evaluator would do better to think of the trial lawyer gathering evidence for a jury or a good investigative reporter looking for corroborating clues to put together a story.

These alternative roles for the evaluator do not dismiss the value of controlled experimental designs, but suggest they be used as a last resort, only when other simpler means fail to gather the evidence necessary to make decisions. Critics may raise the problem of attribution, i.e., by asking how you can prove your project caused the changes you are measuring. But more important is to keep methods simple in each case and to see the general patterns which emerge from the evaluation of a number of small projects.

Equally important reasons for keeping our methods uncomplicated are costs and, returning to our first point, participation. As Richard Johnson warned at the Wingspread Conference, "If you spend money on evaluation you are not spending money on your programs." Complicated methodologies raise costs.

Finally, we return to participation. We began by asserting that PVOs have ample reason to encourage the community's participation in evaluation. Our methods should reflect this belief. Our most creative challenge is to work with participants to develop simple tools to collect and analyze information. In Section II, we provide descriptions and examples of such tools. In general, we must perfect our use of qualitative tools, such as observation, interviews and community meetings, to enrich our information gathering. At the same time, PVOs should devise every means possible to make evaluation meaningful to project participants. This should be a hallmark of PVO methodology.

Evaluation in the Context of Program Design
The next step is to place evaluation within our program procedures. Many assume that the first step in the program development process is identifying the problems faced by an organization's clients. The second is assumed to be developing a program plan for addressing those problems. Only after implementation of the program do practitioners believe that effective methods of evaluation are to be employed. But the perspective of program development as a linear process whose end point is an evaluation phase has been superceded by the understanding that planning and evaluation are inextricably linked: Evaluation is part of planning and planning is part of evaluation.

In this context, evaluation becomes the mechanism by which planners and administrators monitor a program from its inception to completion. By contrast, when evaluation is viewed as a "last phase" of program development, little serious assessment of the foregoing program quality actually occurs, since the organization tends to focus on subsequent program plans. Evaluations have been conducted, for the main part, informally and intuitively, and the findings not rigorously used in the program development process. Tightening standards of accountability, however, have increased the demand for information about program effectiveness. Such information is most likely to be available if the mechanisms for evaluation are set in place as part of the original plan at the outset of the program.

The presence (or absence) of an evaluation strategy at the planning stage is a reflection of the organization's program plan. Rigorous planning involves the incorporation of an evaluation component that will provide information to be used on an ongoing basis to monitor the progress of the program. The evaluation component serves as a measure for effectiveness of the program.

It would be unrealistic to assume that this type of program development is typical for the PVO, or any other, community. On the contrary, we have all observed programs that have "happened" rather than been planned, but the occurence of such "happenings" may be decreasing. Plans with built-in evaluative mechanisms are being increasingly recognized as critical to effective program development and management, as well as necessary for the accurate final assessment of the program's effectiveness.

Uses of Evaluation

Evaluation strategies vary with the different purposes they are intended to serve. No "all-purpose" evaluation is possible, since the way in which evaluation findings are to be used determines the questions that will be posed.

1. *Decision-Making.* Program developers can use evaluation findings to obtain information in order to make better decisions. Evaluation results may help determine whether to continue a program, to add or drop a program component, or to institute a similar program in another context. Health workers, for example, may develop a maternal and child health care program in one community to see if it is effective in reducing infant mortality. If successful, a decision may be made to expand the program to other communities. Alternatively, a different strategy may be developed if the program tested proves ineffectual.

2. *Assessment/Improvement of Performance.* Information from evaluations may be used to identify weak points within a program. By locating the aspects of a program that need modification, the program developer has the ability to make the existing program more effective.

3. *Allocation of Resources.* Neither all programs nor every aspect of a

single program are equally effective in bringing about desired change. An analysis of a program may reveal that one part of its strategy is successful (as defined by the program's objectives) while another is not. An evaluation may show, for example, that a radio broadcast featuring appropriate agricultural innovations for a region has not resulted in the adoption of these new technologies. It may also reveal that the radio broadcasts were effective when used in combination with study groups led by village level agricultural extension workers. The implication for planners may be that more resources should be directed toward the training of village level agricultural workers and less allocated to media presentations.

4. *Personnel Development.* Evaluation results may suggest the relative effectiveness of staff involved in a program. Appropriately developed evaluation questions may also identify training needs that might be addressed through in-service training; they may even suggest the kinds of persons who should be recruited in the future.

5. *Program Justification.* Increasing pressure has been exerted by funding agencies on PVOs to justify program expenditures. The existence of an evaluation strategy will demonstrate that an agency is concerned with issues of effectiveness and committed to improve performance. An evaluation may also show financial supporters whether or not the program results warrant the investment they have made in the program.

6. *Determination of Policy.* Organizations are not only concerned with program results, but also with evaluating their basic strategies and policies. Information gathered through carefully structured evaluations may tell administrators whether the structures and mechanisms that have been developed are appropriate for the task as defined by the organization's policies.

7. *New Knowledge and Understanding.* Most of what is known about the process of development was learned through experience in the field, not in the laboratory. Evaluations can provide a rigorous test of these lessons learned and suggest some generalizations that may be of use to other practitioners. Practitioners will have more confidence in the findings if they are the result of a systematic evaluation process.

Beyond Information Gathering
Evaluations, as the previous section has shown, can help PVOs improve the quality of their programs. For a variety of reasons, however, evaluation findings frequently are not translated into practice.

Where evaluations are planned and implemented by members of the program staff, for example, there is a vested interest in success. The staff may therefore unintentionally overlook problems that have been identified or simply explain them away on the assumption that they have a better picture of the whole program than the ones conducting the evaluation. Similarly, when outside specialists are engaged to evaluate a program, their own agendas may prevent them from accurately understanding what the program is attempting to achieve. Unfortunately, their findings and conclusions may reflect a different set of values and criteria than those held by the program staff. Not only do such evaluation findings prove unhelpful, they frequently ensure that even the good suggestions will be ignored.

Some evaluations are so comprehensive and the information so voluminous that potential users — planners and administrators — are either intimidated or lack the time required to digest the findings. The reports themselves are too long, contain too many obscure statistics, are poorly written and so couched in qualifiers as to be rendered useless for decision-makers. Rather than identifying the values under which the evaluation is being carried out, many evaluation reports equivocate to the extent that no one is sure what is meant. This is done under the guise of maintaining objectivity.

Finally, timing is a critical factor in realizing the usefulness of evaluation findings. Excellent evaluations based on valid and reliable data may, in retrospect, represent wasted time and money, if decisions based on those findings were necessary before the data could be analyzed.

Most of the material selected for this Sourcebook has been provided by PVO practitioners and their agencies. In this sense it is a collage of the state of our art. It is also an aid for further training. There is no question that thinking evaluatively requires a basic knowledge of certain concepts and skills. Whether training is organized collectively or conducted by each agency individually, it is essential for achieving the standards suggested in this section.

There are no a-b-c prescriptions for "how-to" evaluations nor are there easy evaluation recipes. Rather, this Sourcebook is intended as an inspirational guide to the practitioner, a means of enriching the creative evaluation process and catalyzing the PVO community and the people we serve in the Third World.

NOW YOU ARE READY TO EVALUATE

CHAPTER ONE

INTRODUCTION
— THE EVALUATION CLOCK

Our approach is intended to provide fuel to fire creativity without offering a blueprint of the perfect evaluation model. We consider evaluation as an integral part of our working lives and not simply a series of isolated studies doomed to dusty bookshelves. In our view, evaluation contributes directly to an organization's growth and self-understanding. Every PVO should encourage its staff to master the discipline of evaluation and draw on this rich resource for decision-making.

This section suggests evaluation signposts. We begin with the Evaluation clock inspired by the work of Robert E. Stake,[1] and adapted to provide a framework for the evaluation process. The section proceeds through five steps to demonstrate the use of the framework:

1. **In Preparation for the Task:**
   A series of practical guides important to consider even before designing a specific evaluation.

2. **Thinking Through a Strategy for Evaluation:**
   A step-by-step walk through evaluation design using the Evaluation Clock.

3. **The Primary Persuasions:**
   A consideration of the larger evaluation context.

4. **Useful Tools:**
   Briefs suggesting tools to gather information.

5. **Some Thoughts on Utilization:**
   A consideration of effective evaluation utilization.

Throughout this section, we have offered the experiences of agencies each contributing to our concept of an evaluation framework. The ideas in this section, then, represent the collaborative efforts of numerous PVOs.

---

[1]See "Naturalistic Evaluation" in Chapter Four for more information.

Exhibit II-A

THE EVALUATION CLOCK

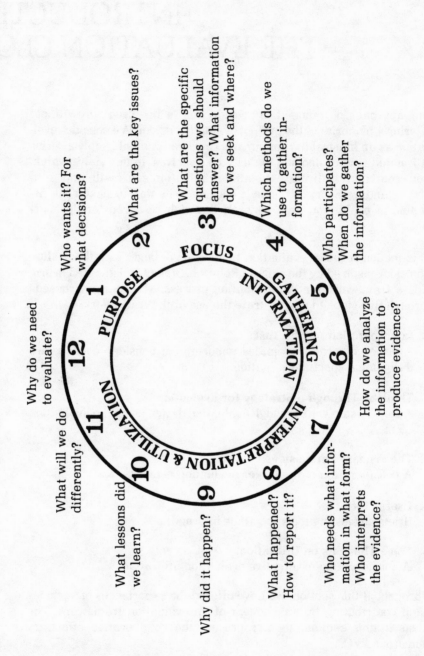

The Evaluation Clock represents the most effective conceptual framework for our purposes. Around the face of the clock are the major
phases of evaluation, broken down into questions that must be answered at some point. The clock marks time in an unusual fashion, since
it does not necessarily move in a clockwise direction, but rather jumps
from one number to another until all the questions have been struck.
So remain calm if seven o'clock comes before two o'clock — it's all
part of the real world of evaluation.

There is an important point to re-emphasize through the clock. Evaluation is most certainly not the last step of the linear process: plan-
action-evaluate. Rather it runs throughout all our work; every time you
sit down with a community group to identify key issues or to discuss the
lessons of past experience, the evaluation clock is set into motion.

Throughout this section the clock symbol will appear, indicating
specific hours. This device provides a simple index guide for those interested in specific questions in the evaluation process.

CHAPTER TWO
IN PREPARATION FOR THE TASK

These are five easy steps toward successful evaluation. Based on actual agency experience, we have prepared a few practical guides which provide useful building blocks for a systematic approach to evaluation.

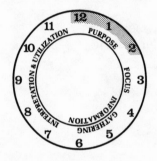

1. Life Cycle of a Project

The project is our starting point because it is the basic management unit for most PVOs. Whether the concept inhibits or encourages communities to organize depends on how we use it.

The following chart depicts an interactive approach for any project. On one level, there are the stages of project development over time; and, on another level is the interaction of principal actors as they impact on the project at different moments of the project's life cycle. There are three principal actors: the COMMUNITY, a group of people working together either because of proximity or common interests; the PVO, an intermediate agency or agencies that provide assistance; and the DONOR, the funding source.

Use this chart as a discussion tool, and add your own modifications. Establishing the purpose of evaluation is easier when the principal actors share an understanding of the project concept.

See accompanying chart

LIFE CYCLE OF A PROJECT

LIFE BEFORE BIRTH	Youth	Adolescence	Adulthood	Middle Age	Old Age	LIFE AFTER DEATH
THE COMMUNITY Its process of development exists already	Youthful exuberance	Identity crisis	Regaining confidence	Renewal of Purpose	Living out the Reality	The Community development process continues.
Gestation period of a plan: After a good idea mates with a community need	The people most affected participate from the first in creating and nourishing this new life	Doubts arise about what the project is achieving	Hard work with rewards not always clear, time for reflection and nourishing ideas	Change for the better perceived; but is it enough?	An extension of life may be needed; if the energy is there.	The impact of a project is immortal. Its last judgment may open the way to a new life.

Evaluation takes form from the day of conception

B A S E L I N E

Frequent checks of vital signs for good health

Keep checking to detect ills early.

JOINTLY	PLANNED	ACTIONS	I M P A C T	TOWARD	DEFINED	OBJECTIVES

MONITORING
"How are we doing?"
A constant dialogue among all involved.

MONITORING
"Are we doing what we wanted?"
See if the flow of benefits reach the right people

F I N A L   E V A L U A T I O N

"What could we do differently?" — Surgery may be needed to prevent early death

"What did we learn?"
— An autopsy or reincarnation assumed by the community

THE PVO

A decision needed... do we continue to support the project? — has our thinking about what is a better life changed? — can we make this project's life more meaningful?

THE DONORS

(where applicable)

They will hold us accountable for our deeds and the use of their resources bequeathed to us.

WARNING

The simplistic logic of many conventional evaluation schemes is anchored in the technocratic project concept, which has grown increasingly sophisticated, demanding and rigid over the years, and further out of touch with reality. Refined technocratic project plans frequently inhibit creativity, spontaneity and the ability to make mid-course corrections and to seize unpredictable targets of opportunity that arise. Evaluations should look for the unexpected, not simply the planned outcomes.

Philip Coombs
Impact Workshop Report,
p. 6. (REF. 1)

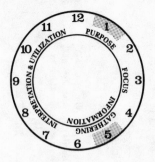

2. A Self-Examination

Entering into the serious business of evaluating others requires a healthy degree of introspection. The following checklists present two levels of analysis: a) assessing practitioners' strength, and b) assessing organization strength.

As a PVO practitioner, you should critically examine your skills and strengths in relation to those needed for evaluation. An analysis of your agency's resources will help you answer the critical *who* questions in the evaluation process.

We suggest you seriously consider these questions before any decisions are made concerning evaluation design or outside evaluation assistance.

See accompanying checklists

a) Assessing Your Strength as an Evaluator

You will want to be sure that your skills and strengths as an evaluator match the needs of the evaluation. The following exercise will assist you in determining if your skills are adequate, or appropriate to a particular situation. For example, if the focus is on a reproduction or breeding problem, perhaps a veterinarian or animal scientist should conduct the evaluation, or be a member of the team. If an organization or a management problem is involved, an evaluator with process skills may be required.

I First, circle the letters that indicate the skills and strengths needed in this evaluation...

II. Next, place an X through the numbers that indicate your own skills and strengths...

		None	Low	Medium	High	Very High
A.	A particular technical expertise. Specify _____	1	2	3	4	5
B.	Problem solving ability.	1	2	3	4	5
C.	Effective writing.	1	2	3	4	5
D.	Getting to the heart of things.	1	2	3	4	5
E.	A language capability. Specify _____	1	2	3	4	5
F.	Cultural understanding and experience.	1	2	3	4	5
G.	Organization.	1	2	3	4	5
H.	Management.	1	2	3	4	5
I.	Statistical analysis.	1	2	3	4	5
J.	Perceptive listening.	1	2	3	4	5
K.	Counseling.	1	2	3	4	5
L.	Understanding of participatory development.	1	2	3	4	5
M.	Linking people, resources, and ideas.	1	2	3	4	5
N.	Others _____ _____	1	2	3	4	5

III. Now compare the skills and strengths *needed* in the evaluation with your *own skills and strengths.* If you have indicated a need for skills and strengths in a particular area, and have rated yourself as a "1" or "2" in the area, you should make sure that a more qualified person is available to assist in that part of the evaluation.

Adapted from *Evaluation Manual,*
Heifer Project International, May 1982,
p. 30. (REF. 2)

(Continues)

b) Assessing Organization Strength

Consider these questions and check the appropriate response:

	Substantial	Some	Very Little	None
a. List skills and strengths needed (Section I of "Assessing your Strength as an Evaluator") Can your organization provide assistance in these areas. 1. 2. 3. 4. 5.				
b. How would you describe the financial resources available for this evaluation?				
b. Do you know who is interested in this evaluation and why?				
d. Will this evaluation provide timely information for your organization's management cycle?				
e. How important is this evaluation to existing agency program policies?				
f. What interest exists in the organization for learning from the evaluation?				

If the answer to any of these questions is "none," effective evaluation is in serious jeopardy. In some cases there may be overriding reasons to proceed, such as the importance of the evaluation to the community. In most cases, however, the practitioner should seek to remedy this perception before going any further. In the case of question "a" outside evaluation assistance may provide an answer. A discussion with colleagues may help with the other questions. Although no evaluation will always rate at the highest levels, beginning an evaluation with weak responses is an invitation to failure.

3. Organizing the Flow of Information

For PVOs, an overriding concern in organizing an evaluation is its utilization. Most agencies do not have the leisure or sufficient funds to conduct evaluation solely for research purposes. To get the most from our investment, an evaluation should satisfy a number of audiences.

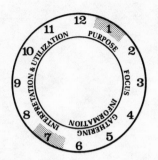

Before deciding on a particular evaluation approach, it is worthwhile to analyze carefully the different audiences. The following matrix, suggested by Robert Bruce at one of our workshops, is a simple tool to organize the task. Astute matching of each audience with the need for information will make the evaluation process more efficient. By using this guide, the PVO practitioner grasps the flow of information required of an evaluation before organizing the specific task itself.

See accompanying matrix

FLOW OF INFORMATION MATRIX

A matrix of this type, adapted to your organization, can help determine how to plan your evaluation; keep in mind the diverse audiences who will use it.

Audiences	Role in Evaluation	Information to Disseminate	Dissemination Format
Outside of Organization (Public, Development Agencies, Local Government, and Donors)	Receive information	Broad lessons learned	Summary journal article Summary report to Donors
Board of Directors	Evaluate information	Lessons learned plus implications for policy	One page brief
PVO Headquarters	Evaluate information and review results; disseminate lessons learned to other regions	Program, operational and administrative; lessons learned have implications for agency policy	Summary plus recommendations; full report available if requested
Regional Office	Review results; decide on implementation of appropriate recommendations	All lessons learned and implications for agency analysis of program progress	Full report; debriefing with outside evaluator (if any)

Country Office	Prepare scope of work (if any); review results, ensure implementation of recommendations, and follow up with project director	Analysis, lessons learned, and implications; all other information not forwarded to regional office and headquarters	Full draft report plus final debriefing with basic evaluation team
Project Director	Active participation in evaluation process; ensure all relevant information is received; implement recommendations	Analysis, lessons learned and implications; all other information not forwarded to regional office and headquarters	Full report; debriefing with all participants in evaluation
Project Participants	Active in evaluation process; analyze progress, contribute to recommendations, and help to carry them out	Analysis; lessons learned and implications for this project and similar ones	Verbal report discussed with all involved in evaluation
Community Members not involved in project	Receive information	Project progress and implications for other community-wide efforts	Via community groups, especially project group and community committee (if any)

Prepared by Peter Van Brunt
Save The Children Federation

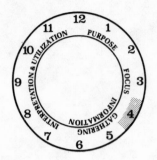

4. Monitoring Information: An Inventory

The importance of monitoring information for systematic evaluation cannot be underestimated. As part of a review of its evaluation system, the American Jewish Joint Distribution Committee undertook an inventory. It gave field staff the following chart as an example, and asked them to provide their own answers using the definition of monitoring developed at our first workshop.

We include this exercise because of its value to PVO management. A community usually has its own, even if informal, methods of monitoring progress. The PVO practitioner might use these questions, perhaps in an open-ended interview, to discover these existing methods. Building on such methods makes the task of designing a participatory evaluation easier. Even an agency that primarily plays a donor role could benefit from knowing the monitoring information its project holders normally gather.

See accompanying chart

MONITORING INFORMATION: AN INVENTORY

Type of Information	Frequency	Who Collects/ Prepares	How do you use for Project Monitoring Management	Information Transmission What and Where	Suggestions for Modification
Statistical reports on new cases, terminated cases, number of home visits	Monthly	Statistician of ABC Health Service	Check data to see that it conforms to expected service levels; if there are any problems or questions, they are asked by letter or on next field visit	Summary data sent to Headquarters	Reduce detail
Statistical summaries of employee work assignments	Monthly	Statistician of ABC Health Service	Check to see that number of staff conforms to contract agreement; questions and problems querried by letter	Include with above	Review periodically and discuss on field trip
Field visits	Varies but about 3 per year	I prepare after my visit and review of programs	General review of situation	Reports sent to Headquarters	No change
Local agency reports	Quarterly	Agency Director has staff prepare notes which are then edited	Read and comment; identify any problems	Not sent out	Wonder if they should be sent out?
Financial Reports on payrolls, supplies, and other expenditures	Quarterly	ABC Health Service's accountant and bookkeeper	Check to see if they are being expended as budgeted; spending in excess query by mail or as part of field visit	Sent with Field Report	Would like to have accountant review and identify necessary information

Prepared by Sherwood Slater, American Jewish Joint Distribution Committee

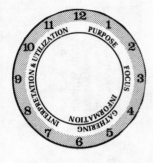

5. Evaluation Design: A Worksheet

In Chapter Two of this section, we use the Evaluation Clock to walk through an evaluation design. The following worksheet, based on that framework, is a guide for organizing your own evaluation design.

Our intent is not to provide a blueprint of the ideal evaluation model, but rather to demonstrate a practical application of an approach that meets the three operating principles described in Section I: participatory approaches, systematic flow of information, and simple but pervasive methodologies. We hope that by suggesting a different perspective on evaluation, this worksheet will further stimulate your own design ideas.

See accompanying worksheet

EVALUATION DESIGN: A WORKSHEET

1. Program/Project:

Hypothetical Project (See Chapter Three of Section II - "Thinking through a Strategy for Evaluation".)

2. List Current Objectives and Resources Invested:
(See Chapter Three)

3. Statement of Purpose (Compile stakeholder concerns to define purpose and identify key issues):

To determine the effectiveness of an innovative community health program in order to decide on its expansion or possible replication elsewhere.

4. Questions Raised by Issues:

- When did critical program decisions pertaining to program operation occur? What were these decisions? How did they influence the program? What other alternatives were or could have been considered? How might have such options affected the program? Who did and/or did not participate in these decisions? How did this affect the program?

- One program component was promotion of home gardening. How did this affect the nutritional status of children under five years of age in participant families?

- One goal of this program was to encourage wider community participation in economic activities. How did the selection of community group leaders affect achievement of this goal?

- Did the participatory training of village workers affect the way they trained villagers?

- Should there be additional voluntary health workers?

(Continues)

5. Key Questions for Evaluation	6. Value Given	7. Sources of Information	8. Tools to Gather Information	9. Who Participates	10. When
1 (program decisions)	Not very important	Staff, Workplans, Proposals, Budgets, Memos, Correspondence, Participants, Donors.	Simple questionnaire for participants; Sample open-ended staff interviews; Tapes of staff meetings; Project document checklist.	Outside evaluator gathers and reviews information with staff.	Mid-term of project
2 (nutritional status)	Important	Children, Mothers.	Arm circumference measure; Scale for weighing; Household observation checklist; Group discussion.	Mothers measure; Staff weighs with mothers; Staff designs with mothers, use during home visit; Mothers organize with staff.	Monthly from beginning; Continuous; Continuous
3 (community participation)	Very important	Community leaders, Community members, Group members, Staff.	Community meetings; Notes of community meetings; Open-ended interviews with community leaders; Survey of participants	Leaders organize/staff assists; Design by community/staff, staff implements; Staff designs with leaders, applied by community volunteers.	Quarterly; Mid-term; Mid-term
4 (participatory training)	Very important	Trainers, Trainees, Syllabi, Group members, Community members.	Workshop evaluation reports; Syllabi checklists; Surveys of participants; Creative expression; Games with participants.	Staff prepares; discuss with community leaders; Teachers apply; Teachers apply; Teachers facilitate; participants perform.	Continuous; Mid-term; Mid-term; Mid-term

11. Plan for an Analysis and Interpretation of Information (Who will be involved and when):

- Staff meets monthly to monitor information gathered on continuous basis.

- At mid-term, evaluator tabulates questionnaire and organizes information from interviews and existing records to provide evidence concerning program decisions.

- Health staff organizes nutrition statistics and consults with health services nutritionist to determine significance. Staff discusses this analysis with mothers to determine relevance.

- Evaluator assists staff and community volunteers to tabulate survey. Staff organizes information from interviews. Trainers prepare reports on workshops.

- Evaluator facilitates an analysis meeting with project staff and community participants to identify important patterns.

12. Use of Evaluation (How to derive lessons and make them available for decision-making):

(See Chapter Three.)

CHAPTER THREE

THINKING THROUGH AN EVALUATION STRATEGY

Evaluation Design for PVO Programs
In terms of organizational structure, PVOs do not differ greatly from other organizations involved in international development. PVOs usually have a headquarters, whether in the United States or in the Third World, an intermediate level of regional or country offices, and, finally, a local organization that supports particular programs. This Sourcebook focuses on the local level, for it is there that evaluation must begin. But local field programs are directly affected by decisions originating from regional or headquarters levels. It is important, therefore, that we see local program evaluation as part of the larger evaluation system.

However, the underlying values of PVOs differentiate them from other development agencies. PVO programs are defined by the following characteristics: directed to the poor; emphasize participation by beneficiaries in planning and decision-making; emphasize process as much as tangible results; demonstrate flexible and innovative approaches to field programs; work with and strengthen local, private institutions; and execute small-scale programs at low cost.[1] These characteristics, and the resulting programs, will strongly influence the methods PVOs utilize while conducting field program evaluations. To better see this in practice, let us walk through the steps of an evaluation design using the Evaluation Clock.

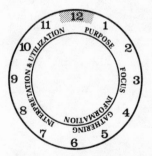

Choosing the Correct Evaluation Design:
Why Do We Need to Evaluate?
PVO evaluations usually try to satisfy simultaneously the expectations of several very different groups:

• Program managers want status reports.

• Policy makers want information relevant to policy and planning decisions.

---

[1]Whether these self-descriptions do in fact characterize PVO programs is discussed in Judy Tendler, "Turning PVOs Into Development Agencies: Questions for Evaluation". *AID Program Evaluation Discussion Paper No. 12* (April 1982). (Ref. 5)

- Donors want to know about program impact and whether their funds were well invested.

- Field staff seek to determine program effectiveness, required modifications, and identify problems regarding staffing and administration.

- The affected community, too often the last to be considered, wants to know how the program responds to its needs.

These sometimes competing concerns provide ample motivation to evaluate, but they tend to complicate the challenge we face: to match the PVO with an appropriate evaluation design.

Exhibit II-B

PVO Experience: World Education, Inc.

Designing an Evaluation that Fits:

One example of how evaluation focus and methodology can vary over the life of a program is found in a current World Education project with Tototo Home Industries in Mombasa, Kenya. This project assists groups of rural women through nonformal education to establish cottage industries and small-scale economic enterprises. The project started in 1977 and will end in 1985; three separate types of evaluation will have been conducted by the end of eight years.

The first evaluation sought to measure the effects of nonformal education on the process of group formation and group ability to plan and implement economic activities. It used a mix of management and social science methods — facilitator logs, community surveys, in-depth interviews, and project records. Social science methods were used at three points to collect data: pre-program, a mid-point, and post-program. Management information was collected continuously and analyzed at the same time as the "scientific" data. The nonformal education method was found effective and the program expanded.

The second evaluation of the expanded phase focuses primarily on program monitoring; data are collected continuously and analyzed quarterly so that program staff share understandings of problems and successes, and deviations from workplans and timetables are justified.

A third evaluation of this program will be exclusively directed to answering the following question: "Do income generation projects for women significantly raise family income and, if so, does this income have an effect on women's fertility?" This evaluation will only utilize social science research methods and design and will not concern itself with management issues.

(Continues)

The point of this example is to demonstrate that no evaluation can be all things to all people, and in order to know what data to collect and what methods to use to collect them, you must know what questions need answers. This project will remain essentially unchanged for eight years. The first evaluation determined that a particular educational method was effective in fostering group cohesion and group decision-making. It could not provide answers to the question raised by the third evaluation — how do these programs affect family income and fertility — because it was not designed to answer those questions. It could provide answers to questions raised in the second evaluation — how are we doing? — because in order to know whether the educational method was effective, the evaluators had to be sure that the program was implemented efficiently and that any possible failure in the method was due to the method itself and not to a badly-run program.

The second evaluation provides management information to the program staff. It points out staffing problems, resource constraints, communications difficulties, failures and successes of training curricula. This evaluation is the most limited in scope and therefore the easiest to do; it is also the most essential. It cannot provide answers to questions raised by the first and third evaluation: it assumes the questions answered by the first evaluation — does this method work? — can still be answered "yes," since it is the same program, the same population, and the same staff. It does not presume to answer questions raised by the third evaluation because those questions are beyond its scope.

The third evaluation provides information for development donors and policy makers at large: does an effective program using a tested educational method and implemented in a well-organized manner affect certain variables — income and fertility — that we as donors and politicians are concerned with? This evaluation assumes what has already been shown: the method works, and the program operates efficiently. It relies on the two previous evaluations but does not duplicate them.

The choice of evaluation methods was determined by the evelation questions and ranged from basic program monitoring and management techniques to sophisticated sociological research. The questions themselves were determined by PVO concerns at three separate periods. First the two PVOs wanted to know if a method was successful in order to decide whether to expand or revise a program. Next, the PVOs wanted to insure that the expansion was proceeding as planned. Finally, the donors wanted to know if such a program had additional benefits that warranted the promotion and support of similar programs elsewhere. In all three evaluations, the needs of the PVOs for specific information dictated the choice of evaluation methodology, and thus a fit or match was achieved between information requirements and evaluation methodology.

Prepared by Jeanne McCormack,
World Education Inc.

Program Evaluation and Information Needs

The practice of evaluation is the result of a peculiar convergence between organizational management and social science research. In Chapter Four of this section we will examine this convergence in more detail. When we speak of PROGRAM MONITORING and the need for evaluation as aids to decision making, we draw upon those aspects of evaluation methodology derived from the "science" of management. However, when we speak of IMPACT EVALUATION, we refer to methods and approaches rooted in educational and sociological research. The line between program evaluation, the generic term for evaluation activities that includes both management and social science approaches, and evaluation research, which generally focuses on program outcomes and utilizes social science research methods, is a fine one. The particular mix of methods an organization utilizes in evaluation should depend on the specific purpose of the evaluation.

Defining Purpose: Who Wants It? For What Decisions?

In thinking through a program evaluation strategy, it is first necessary to list the concerns of the STAKEHOLDERS. These stakeholders are the interested parties and include the community, staff, headquarters managers, and donors.

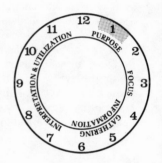

Many concerns should be apparent at the project's preliminary planning stage, and these may relate to specific project objectives. Other concerns might arise during the course of program implementation. One way to enumerate project concerns is to convene a group of principal stakeholders and together hammer out a list of essential questions. If the list is too long, the group can rank the concerns by importance and come up with a list of manageable size. A clearly determined purpose makes all other evaluation tasks easier.

Exhibit II-C

Some Ideas on How to Define the Purpose

In defining the purpose of an evaluation it is important to identify and consult with certain key people, such as administrators, project managers, etc. It is also recommended that donors, interested third parties, and project leaders at the community level be included whenever possible. They should be asked to consider and respond to the question, "Do we need to do an evaluation, and why?" Their responses should be summarized in a written statement of purpose which will be the guide for conducting the evaluation.   (Continues)

Additional methods for defining the purpose of an evaluation include:
- Surveying the needs for an evaluation by asking key people to respond in writing to an open ended phrase such as, "We need to evaluate this project so that...."
- If it is not possible to get responses in writing, interview key people focusing on the "so that" phrase or similar questions.
- Fill out an "Evaluation Work-Up" sheet with those who are requesting the evaluation.
- Meet with the project team (those staff and project personnel who are most heavily involved in the project). Discuss the questions on the Work-Up sheet and attempt to arrive at a consensus.
- Consult with all those in decision-making positions whose approval and/or support is essential to the process, and those who will be using the results.

It is usually more practical to carry out individual interviews with these "key people" asking each to consider the question, "What decisions should we be able to make after having completed the evaluation?" Always be aware of possible "hidden agendas," i.e., reasons for conducting the evaluation which may be outside the scope of the project or which focus on a "special interest" situation.

It is suggested that the persons responsible for organizing the evaluation review the original project description, the established goals and objectives, the amount of resources which have been invested in the project, and any reports and observations which may have already been written about the project. After making this review and consulting with the key people on the project, it should be possible to write a concise statement of the need for and purpose of the evaluation.

Adapted from *Evaluation Manual*, Heifer
Project International, 1982, p. 5. (REF. 2)

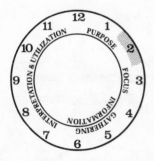

Inputs vs. Impact: What are the Key Issues?
PVOs too often stress inputs to the exclusion of process and impact in their evaluations. Such an approach might show, for example, that the program money arrived on time, a given number of beneficiaries participated, the drop-out rate was at a certain level, a certain number of staff were trained, or that various materials were produced. Whether this occurs because of poorly stated objectives or difficulty gathering sufficient information, the evalution will fail to provide information on program impact. To make evaluation a useful tool, we must avoid this trap.

In this phase of evaluation design, it is essential *not* to limit yourself solely to a quantitative measurement of how effectively a program achieves its objectives. Rather, our framework starts from an awareness of the full range of stakeholders' concerns (see *Evaluation Design*

Worksheet, items 1-4). By clustering individual concerns, it is possible to identify a number of KEY ISSUES. These issues illustrate the complexity one generally faces at this point. From these issues, PVO practitioners can derive questions that move beyond inputs, and focus their evaluation efforts on realistic goals.

To illustrate, let us consider a hypothetical program evaluation. A PVO compiles stakeholder concerns into a statement of purpose (Worksheet Item 3) to determine the effectiveness of an innovative community health program in order to decide on its expansion or possible replication elsewhere. An identification of key issues leads to the following questions under worksheet item four:

Question # 1. When did critical program decisions pertaining to program operation occur? What were these decisions? How did they influence the program? What other alternatives were or could have been considered? How might have such options affected the program? Who did and/or did not participate in these decisions? How did this affect the program?

Question # 2. One program component was promotion of home gardening. How did this affect the nutritional status of children under five years of age in participant families?

Question # 3. One goal of this program was to encourage wider community participation in economic activities. How did the selection of community group leaders affect achievement of this goal?

Question # 4. Did the participatory training of village workers affect the way they trained villagers?

Question # 5. Should there be additional voluntary health workers?

Finding a Focus: What Are the Specific Questions We Should Answer?

The next step is to determine which questions *should* be answered given the time and the resources available for evaluation. Evaluation provides information needed by an organization to make decisions. But what kind of *decisions* and what kind of *information*?

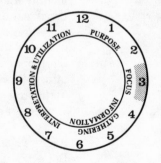

Each day, PVOs make a multitude of decisions which do not depend upon evaluation results. For example, the decision to add an extra volunteer community health worker to a program can be made by talking to villagers, to staff, or by reading field worker reports. The information necessary to make the decision is easily available and does not require a formal education. However, the decision to establish a village health training program is not so easy. Concerning this issue, an evaluation can provide substantial new information and, thereby, inform more rational decision making.

Value of Information

These examples suggest that certain kinds of information are more valuable than others. Information is valuable if it is new or previously unknown. It is even more valuable if knowing it is likely to directly influence organization decision making.

The information provided by a full-scale evaluation of, for example, the adequacy of volunteers will probably not change the organization's future because it is not new; people already know the strengths and deficiencies of the system in an informal way. But an evaluation of community awareness and acceptance of a health training program may uncover some surprises and, therefore, affect the kind of programs an organization undertakes in the future.

Cost of Information

Directly related to the value of information is its cost. By cost we mean not merely money spent, but work performed, hopes raised, and time used. No organization should devote more time and effort to getting information than the information is worth. Let us look at an example where the cost of the evaluation is high but the cost of going without it is even higher.

Suppose a credit organization believes that residents of a rural area do not use their services to farmers because they are unaware of this service. To remedy this need, the organization institutes an intensive education campaign publicizing the service. The campaign lasts three months and relies primarily on radio announcements. At the end of three months, an evaluation indicates that community awareness has not increased. A more careful investigation shows that three-quarters of the residents of this rural area have no radio and were therefore unable to hear the advertisements. The cost of not knowing this information was indeed high, much higher than the cost of collecting it in the first place. The organization paid the price of wasted resources, lost time, and great disappointment.

Factors Determining Focus

Determining which question *should* be answered depends on these factors:

- The organization's resources. Does the organization have the money, expertise, and time to answer the question, particularly if it requires research procedures?

- The consequences of making a wrong decision. If the decision results in commitment of a large amount of resources for a significant period, it is important that the decision be made wisely. The organization should rely on more than just hunches, intuition, judgement, and opinions.

- The organization's knowledge of the true state of affairs. Has it determined, through informal evidence, that a particular goal is being attained? Does the organization expect some surprises? The likelihood of uncovering new or unknown information is an important factor in the decision to conduct a rigorous evaluation.

- What are the external requirements? PVO evaluations often include answering questions for funding agencies. Evaluation can, therefore, be viewed as part of the program to secure resources that insure the program's continued survival. This orients evaluation to certain kinds of decisions, such as those relating to a program's continuation.

With this in mind, we can begin to address the second part of our Evaluation Design Worksheet. Let us assume that we decide to focus on the first four questions (page 43) in assessing our hypothetical program. Assume the program has gone extremely well; the PVO staff is pleased, the community enthusiastically supports the program, the donors are impressed. The evaluation team could therefore conclude that since no major problems have been encountered in the program, they will look for information concerning critical program decisions only if it is easily obtainable. In essence this question is interesting but not vital to any stakeholder in the program.

Participation, however, is a major concern of the program. Therefore, it is important to consider key Question #3 (i.e., community participation) and key Question #4 (i.e. participatory training), since both impact on community participation. Nutritional status (key Question #2) as an outcome indicator is of some importance although not as much as evidence about participation. Items [5] and [6] of this PVO worksheet would look like this:

[5.] Key Questions	[6.] Value Given
#1 (program decisions)	Not very important
#2 (nutritional status)	Important
#3 (community participation)	Very important
#4 (participatory training)	Very important

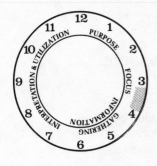

Setting the Information Snares:
What Information Do We Seek and Where?

The next step in planning an evaluation strategy is to determine what information exists and is available. To find answers to the first set of questions (program decisions), most organizations have a wealth of sources of information: staff members, workplans, budgets, correspondence, memos, proposals, and reports. Although we can imagine a critical situation — one marked by high staff turnover, high rate of participant dropout, sketchy documentation, or few information sources — this is, we hope, a rare exception.

Question #2 (nutritional status) can be answered only if there is a way to compare children's nutritional status *before* and *after* implementation of the program. One must also determine that whatever change occurred took place as a result of the program and not because of other reasons. These are measurement and design problems, and, in principle, there are two sources of information — mothers and children. Community members, program participants, and staff could provide information on Questions #3 and #4. Trainers, community workers, and comunity members could furnish additional information on Question #4. Adding Item [7], the Worksheet looks as follows:

[5.] Key Questions	[6.] Value Given	[7.] Sources of Information
#1 (program decisions)	Not very important	Staff Workplans Proposals Budgets Memos Correspondence Participants Donors
#2 (nutritional status)	Important	Children Mothers
#3 (community participation)	Very important	Community leaders Community members Groups members Staff

[5.] Key Questions	[6.] Value Given	[7.] Sources of Information
#4 (participatory training)	Very important	Trainers Trainees Syllabi Group members Community members

Exhibit II-D

A PVO EXPERIENCE : Community Housing Project

Looking back at our attempts to create participatory evaluation mechanisms for these projects, there are some important lessons to be learned.

For instance, we believed an important monitoring tool for each construction group was to keep careful track of hours worked by each participant. The Zambian approach diverged from this type of measure, however, toward one that made allowances for particular circumstances, nuances of behavior, and the attitudes of each group member. The result was a significant shift: Western expectations yielded to Zambian norms.

The first building groups went through the motions of keeping track of hours on the time record sheet kept by the timekeeper; but they generally passed responsibility for timekeeping to the construction teachers. The first group experienced tensions over work hours within two weeks after building began. Some members were, according to the record at least, not pulling their weight; but the group deferred imposing sanctions against the slackers and decided to use the time record sheet merely as a public record of what each family was contributing. After ten weeks the first group was so dissatisfied with this method of accounting for family contributions that it asked for the recording of man-hours to be stopped. Despite staff requests that they continue recording hours, the first group eliminated this procedure and with it the basic premise of the Work Exchange Agreement. Nevertheless construction teachers did continue to record aggregate group hours.

After abandoning the man-hour concept, families continued to work together despite differences in family contribution as great as 500 hours, and despite the fact that groups never called on slackers to pay the penalty charged for hours not worked. Moreover, the earliest project participants advised later building groups not to expel lazy members and not to worry about the actual number of hours contributed.

Why was this so? The reasons probably stemmed from the homebuilders' own social values and norms. According to their view a participant's attitude, not the number of hours worked, was the important consideration. A share of the work cannot be quantified.

"Urban Self-Help Housing," *Monitoring Workshop Report*, p. 59. (REF. 1)

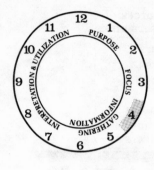

Quantitative and Qualitative Methods:
Which Methods Do We Use to Gather Information?

Methods for collecting information for evaluation are also the subject of Chapter Five of this section.

Evaluators have traditionally emphasized quantitative data when determining program impact. They have relied on social science research methods. There are many valid technical objections to a total reliance on quantitative methods. But more important than purely technical issues, PVOs may be neither equipped nor inclined to use such methods. Furthermore, if quantitative methods are used exclusively, we may miss the richness provided by qualitative data that allows us to interpret quantitative data. Reliance on quantitative methods may also engender cultural resistance in societies less number-oriented than our own as Exhibit II-D illustrates.

The distinction between qualitative and quantitative information is often misleading. Ultimately, the validity of information depends on how persuasive it is to evaluation audiences. For the small-scale community programs that most PVOs operate, notes or tapes of carefully selected participant group discussions may be just as valid, and certainly more compatible, than a full-scale survey using a closed-ended, computer-coded questionnaire. The choice of methods depends on what you want to know about a program as well as what produces the desired results. In most instances, this criteria means a mixture of qualitative and quantitative methods that cross-validate each other.

With this in mind, the next item now can be filled in:

[5.] Key Questions	[6.] Value Given	[7.] Sources of Information	[8.] Tools to Gather Information
#1 (program decisions)	Not very important	Staff Workplans, etc.	Simple questionnaire for participants; Sample open-ended staff interviews; Tapes of staff meetings; Project document checklist.

[5.] Key Questions	[6.] Value Given	[7.] Sources of Information	[8.] Tools to Gather Information
#2 (nutritional status)	Important	Children Mothers	Arm circumference measure; Household observation checklist; Scale for weighing children; Group discussion not with mothers.
#3 (community participation)	Very important	Community leaders and members, etc.	Notes of community meetings; Open-ended interviews with community leaders; Survey of participants.
#4 (participatory training)	Very important	Trainers Trainees, Syllabi, etc.	Workshop evaluation reports; Syllabi checklists; Survey of participants; Games with participants.

Specifying the Methods: Who Participates and When Do We Gather the Information?

When deciding on the methods to be used, the variables "who" and "when" are often considered simultaneously. In this Sourcebook, our preference for involving the communities in evaluation design and implementation processes is clear. The requirement of "objectivity" (i.e. outside, value-free assessment) is sometimes raised against self- or participatory-evaluation. By making clear the soundness, or what a researcher would call "confirmability," of our information we can allay this objection. If designed properly, the participatory approach can benefit from an outside evaluator.

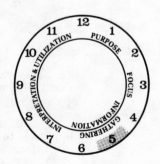

Exhibit II-E

Gathering Information

Two considerations to keep in mind when deciding how to undertake this task:

The methods must be compatible with the values, understandings, and capabilities of those who are being asked to provide information. What has been said earlier about cultural and interpersonal sensitivity is especially true now, for it is only with an understanding of the social and cultural, and often political, environment that the "best way" to go about collecting data can be determined.

The process of data collection may, itself, be a negative influence on the project and the people involved. "Evaluation" makes people nervous. The information collection process should be conducted in as positive a manner as possible for the benefit of the project participants. The act of asking questions, if done in a negative manner, could raise anxiety, decrease trust, and cause people to become discouraged. On the other hand, if done in a positive manner, it can clarify thinking, build trust and motivate people to greater effort. For example, some questions raise expectations, and help people to start rethinking needs, solutions, and goals. In like manner, periodic checking (or monitoring) can be useful in giving encouragement and in building trust and team spirit. Also, a summative evaluation at the end of the project can help staff and community to reflect on where they have been and what they have accomplished.

In summary:
"Methods must be compatible with the cultures represented, a variety of methods are often more appropriate and more productive than a single one, precision and simplicity are essential, methods of evaluation enhance or hinder learning, control groups are desirable although not necessary, the (evaluators) must be clear as to their own objectives in doing the evaluation and can encourage the cooperation of participants by explaining the objectives to them."[1]

– George W. Renwick, Evaluation Handbook — For Cross Cultural Education *(La Grange Park, IL: Intercultural Network), p. 18.*

Adapted from Evaluation Manual, *Heifer Project International, 1982, p. 13. (REF. 2)*

Continuing with our example, let us focus on Worksheet items 8, 9, and 10 and outline how we gather information.

[8.] Tools to Gather Information	[9.] Who Participates	[10.] When
Questionnaire Staff interviews Tapes, Staff meetings Checklists	Outside evaluator gathers and reviews information with staff	Mid-term of project

[8.] Tools to Gather Information	[9.] Who Participates	[10.] When
Arm circumference Scale for weighing	Mothers measure Staff weighs with mothers	Monthly from beginning
Household observation	Staff designs with mothers, use during home visit	Continuous
Group discussion	Mothers organize with staff	Continuous
Community meeting notes	Leaders organize/ staff assists	Quarterly
Interviews	Design by community/ staff; staff implements	Mid-term
Survey	Staff designs with leaders; applied by community volunteers	Mid-term
Workshop reports	Staff prepares; discuss with community leaders	Continuous
Syllabi checklists	Teachers apply	Mid-term
Surveys	Teachers apply	Mid-term
Games with participants	Teachers facilitate; participants perform	Mid-term

A Participatory System

The participatory approach has definite implications for when information is gathered. Information becomes available depending on the community's schedule rather than that of an outside researcher. The PVO evaluator often must negotiate this question among his diverse audiences. Ideally, evaluation is planned from the conception of a project idea. This early foresight is important since every evaluation effort can benefit from pre- and post-project information. In our example, Question #2 requires some comparative information if any compelling evidence is to be developed concerning the project's impact on nutritional status.

A good part of our evaluation design stresses monitoring project development. At the end of two years, or mid-term, an outside evaluator, who mostly facilitates the process, comes in and, together with project staff, gathers the relevant monitoring information. In addition, interviews are conducted with the surveys. This compilation of information from various sources provides an ample "data" base upon which to

---

Exhibit II-F

Making the Participatory Approach Work

Some operating principles for evaluators:
- accompany the team implementing the project with a certain frequency, on their field trips, program meetings, administrative events, etc.
- look for and organize information concerning advances and blockages the project experiences
- help assure the project team a regular flow of information concerning the different phases the project passes through
- analyze all data jointly
- encourage collective reflection opportunities to analyze accomplishments, failures and alterations of work plans and propose needed corrective measures
- present periodically a synthesis to the project team. . .(of evaluative observations).

> Adapted in translation from "Participatory Evaluation of Social Development Projects," by Tito Quiros, *Solidarios*, July-September, 1981, p. 7. (REF. 2)

---

build an analysis for answering the crucial last four questions of the Evaluation Clock. The point to remember is the importance of *systematic* gathering of information. Evaluation is not a sporadic study of events, but rather a purposeful, continuous activity in which all the principal actors participate and, hopefully, benefit.

Keeping Analysis Simple:
How Do We Analyze the Information to Produce Evidence?

Evaluation analysis is often associated with complicated statistics and cost-benefit calculations. We do not deny the importance of advanced techniques of statistical inquiry. It is possible, however, to be just as valid using simple techniques that are within the reach of the average PVO staff person, and, more importantly, the members of communities we work with.

This phase of the Evaluation Clock requires three steps in using information:

1. **EDIT** — weed out irrelevant information or obvious mistaken responses;
2. **TABULATE** — where applicable, develop quantifiable data that demonstrates a relationship or trend;
3. **ARRANGE** — organize information so that quantitative and qualitative data illuminates the question investigated, and is easily

understood. The information should point out changes in the broader context of the project as well as specific changes related to project objectives.

Much has been written about the mechanics of tabulating surveys or content analysis of interviews. (A sample is indicated in the Sourcebook bibliography.) The PVO practitioner should be acquainted with these techniques, and not underestimate their creative potential. The product of our analysis is *evidence*, the refined information that helps to answer the evaluation focus questions.

Exhibit II-G

A PVO Experience: Peasant Organizations

This evaluation experience involving a group of peasant organizations suggests even tabulation can be a highly creative tool:

Once these preliminary plans for the scope and the objectives of the evaluation were agreed upon we began the task of the questionnaire. The first suggestion from the group was to divide into groups according to organizational affiliation so that those who were most familiar with each organization's program would be working on the definition of their goals and the description of their means. They felt that this would be the most expedient approach. But because one of the goals of the evaluation was to coordinate activities between organizations and programs, it was suggested that we work through each program as a group so that the members from each organization would begin to know the other program in detail. It would be an exchange of vocabulary and definition as well as purpose.

By the end of the first week a compact questionnaire had been designed. It was decided that all of the communities would be included in the evaluation. Because we had designed the questionnaire as a group, that is, not broken up into groups by organization to produce separate questionnaires, any member of the group could go to a community to conduct the interview/discussion. In this way the approximately 20 leaders at the regional level could easily cover the seventy communities in the evaluation. It also meant that all of the regional leaders would have heard the statement of members and leaders of all of the organizations in at least some of the communities. They felt that in four weeks all of the interviews could be done and so that two months later, just prior to the end of the year, I should return to assist with the tabulation and analysis. This fit into the national framework of year-end reviews of the organizations and this region would have a concise and studied position paper to present at the planning sessions for the coming year.

Upon return at the end of the year it was found that they had carried out the study as planned. A few communities had not been covered, but a few which had not been on the initial list were later identified and brought into the study. Upon final typing of the questionnaire they had discovered omissions and questions that did not seem ade-

(Continues)

quate, and they had changed them accordingly. These changes indicated that they were thoughtfully working on the task at hand and that they had maintained a critical attitude toward group work. There was no mystery behind "evaluation technology".

In the tabulation process we used simple frequencies at first to compare responses across organizations and to see what the regional strengths and weaknesses were. We were also able to identify communities with specific problems and make note of them for the coming year's promotional activities. The tabulation stage, which is often processed by machine, or personnel not involved with analysis, also became a session for analysis. We were able to discuss conditions in specific communities because the person who had conducted the interview/discussion was there to relate more details. Also, where there was more than one organization in a given community, the regional team had at least one member who had been working with that community and a more thorough analysis could be carried out.

> Adapted from "Participation in Evalua-
> tion at a Regional Level," by Kris
> Merschrod, *Impact Workshop Report*,
> pp. 79-81. (REF. 1)

Turning back to the Worksheet, we need to complete item [11], "Plan for an Analysis and Interpretation of Information." This item outlines the type of analysis needed and who will do it:

- Staff meets monthly to monitor information gathered on continuous basis.

- At mid-term, evaluator tabulates questionnaire and organizes information from interviews and existing records to provide evidence concerning program decisions.

- Health staff organizes nutrition statistics and consults with health services nutritionist to determine significance. Staff discusses this analysis with mothers to determine relevance.

    - Evaluator assists staff and community volunteers to tabulate survey. Staff organizes information from interviews. Trainers prepare reports on workshops.

    - Evaluator facilitates an analysis meeting with project staff and community participants to identify important patterns.

Who Needs What Information in What Form?
Who Interprets the Evidence?
When beginning to interpret evidence, the "who" question becomes critical once again. As suggested earlier,

Exhibit II-H

A PVO Experience: Overseas Education Fund

The OEF is developing an evaluation system that offers a helpful perspective on how to analyze and interpret evaluative information:

Evaluation is carried out during a project by a "project steering committee." The committee is formed during project planning or project initiation and typically includes members of the local organization(s), representatives from among the project participants, and the OEF technical advisor (totalling about four to six people). On a monthly basis, the committee is designated to meet to discuss "how the project's going" in relation to the workplan. The monthly meetings provide a forum for identifying and solving problems, for considering task assignments, and, generally, for assuring the project is on track. We've found simple ratings of project activities to be a good way to stimulate discussion and analysis. For example, committee members each assign a number from one to ten to a particular project activity as a means to indicate their views of its effectiveness. Then, discussion follows on why individuals chose these ratings.

The midpoint evaluation follows a specific process that has been refined through the experience of seven projects. The process includes three major phases: A Design Workshop, Data Collection, and A Data Analysis/Recommendations Workshop. Completion of the three phases takes from two to three weeks, and this considerable time demand appears to be one of the major challenges of using the approach.

An "evaluation facilitator," usually hired by OEF/Washington in consultation with the field, coordinates the midpoint evaluation. The role of this person is to involve an "evaluation team," composed of the steering committee and other individuals the committee designates (between six and ten individuals), in carrying out their own evaluation of project activities. The initial *Design Workshop* (one day) creates a shared viewpoint of the evaluation by beginning with a look at "what is evaluation" and then moving to the definition of "what will be evaluated?," "how?," "by whom?," and "by when?" For the *Data Collection* phase, most projects have utilized interviews, questionnaires, review of documents, observation, and group discussion. OEF is currently exploring other ways to collect data, in particular, ways that require minimal literacy skills. The *Data Analysis/Recommendations Workshop* (one-two days) is the time the data collected is reported and discussed. The emphasis in this workshop is action: "What have we learned about the project so far, and what does that tell us about ways to strengthen the implementation plan in the next phase/year?"

Throughout the three-phase process, the evaluation facilitator guides the analysis of the project and adds insights from his/her own experience. This individual is not a disinterested observer nor an ultimate judge of project effectiveness. Rather, the evaluation facilitator serves both as a challenger of the team members' points of view and as mediator of different points of view. A task of the facilitator may be to convince, but not to impose.

Adapted from Suzanne Kindervatter.
"Striving for an Ideal: The OEF
Participatory Evaluation System," 1982.
(REF. 2)

you should seriously bear in mind the stakeholders' concerns even before designing an evaluation plan. At 1:00 on our Evaluation Clock, you explored the concerns of diverse stakeholders at the start of your planning. You return to them now because *people are at the heart of the evaluation process!* An experienced evaluator wants to establish a dialogue with stakeholders throughout an evaluation. This helps gain credibility in two important ways. First, dialogue with stakeholders — particularly PVO decision-makers and donors — assures their concurrence in the evaluation design. Secondly, involvement of the community acts as a check on the evidence revealed by analysis.

In order to address this point refer back to the "Matrix for Organizing the Flow of Information" on page 30, and review the last two Columns: "Information to Disseminate" and "Dissemination Format."

The Heart of the Evaluation Process

The next four questions on our Evaluation Clock are the very heart of the evaluation process. They include what happened, why it happened, lessons learned, and what to do differently.

At this point, standard evaluation texts often either drift into platitudes about how the evaluator's work is completed, once the final report is turned in, and the rest depends on the decision-maker; or the texts discuss complicated theories of evaluation utilization. In our view, PVOs are blessed by relatively uncomplicated bureaucracies. Most PVOs have little difficulty in achieving the level of communication among their staff that an effective use of evaluation requires. These questions, then, suggest a structure to put this advantage to best use.

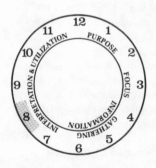

The Communication Factor: What Happened? How to Report It?

The communication factor begins with the organization of evidence to answer the question "What happened?" It is perfectly conceivable that one can conduct evaluations without formal written reports. Where the evaluation is directed to few audiences, all of whom participate fully in each phase, face-to-face discussions may supplant a formal report. In most cases, however, the need to communicate with distant audiences, e.g., headquarters, local government officials or a donor, and with those who have only a fleeting familiarity with a program, requires careful attention to reporting.

Some evaluative reporting occurs as part of ongoing monitoring of a project. The classic PVO *progress report* generally provides information on inputs and a descriptive account of the products/activities resulting from the use of the inputs. Some PVOs wisely build on this type of reporting to include analytical information that goes beyond mere description. The systematic reporting of field staff normal activity, both as a participant observer and interviewer, is a means of gathering evaluative information that each PVO should nurture.

Exhibit II-I

A PVO EXPERIENCE: MAP INTERNATIONAL

Medical Assistance Programs, MAP International, is using a tracking system to provide regular reporting on projects. The centerpiece of the system are codes which the field staff analyzes. MAP is simplifying the form to facilitate its use by other community groups.

Overview: Development assistance often takes the form of project activity. As projects are implemented, it is important to keep track of what is happening. The *Project Tracking System* provides a systematic way to track a number of development projects simultaneously, uniformly, and analytically. The process will aid midcourse attunement of projects, provide information for accountability, and facilitate organizational learning.

Focus: The Project Tracking System focuses on small development projects implemented at the community level by local organizations.

Assumptions: The Project Tracking System assumes the following:
1. Development at the community level has to do with people becoming more able and active in doing something about their own needs.
2. Development is learning. Change within people is more important than change outside people.
3. Learning is a function of reflection which leads to action which then simulates more reflection. Project activities should rise out of community reflection, not externally imposed.
4. Development learning begins long before project activities are initiated.

Critical Indicators: Project success — achieving pre-stated objectives — is not the best indicator of development. Better indicators are:
1. Clusters of self-initiated activities.
2. Local people making development decisions for themselves.
3. Local responsibility and management and decreasing dependence on external personnel and financial resources.
4. Local resource commitment, i.e. money, savings, land, labor, etc.

(Continues)

The Codes Form (six pages long) is designed to track the development of a project according to four central values with three indicators for each value.

1. Complete the Codes Form:
   a. After the first contact (use FCF lines).
   b. After the project investigation (use PIF lines).
   c. When the project plan is completed (use PDF lines).
   d. Every six months after project activities begin.

2. Tailor the codes for each project by writing project-specific codes under the more general codes suggested on the printed form wherever it will enhance clarity of relevance. Agree with project lenders about specific wording for their projects.

3. Use the same form every time you score the project so you will use the same specific codes for every scoring.

4. Use the same form as a guide for semi-annual review discussions with project leaders.

5. Do not limit discussion or observations to these codes. Write other relevant comments on the last page. Add more pages as needed.

The Codes Form is set up in the following manner:

Title _____ No. _____
                          Date activities began _____

A. *Concept Formation.* Are project leaders growing in their understanding of development?

   0 = Vision exists. More enthusiasm than rationale.

   1 = Vision shared and discussed with Regional Director.

   2 = Vision refined. Counsel and/or instruction (e.g. workshop) received and appreciated.

   3 = Vision developmentally sound. Project leaders reflect together and are growing in their under-

	Mo/Yr	Score
FCF		
PIF		
PDF		

The complete Codes Form includes the following questions, each with answers ranked 0 to 3:

B. *Design and Evaluation.* Is the plan written, reviewed and revised?

C. *Funding.* Are resources available so the project can proceed as planned?

(Continues)

PROJECT ACTIVITIES

D. *Community Education*. Are local people learning what they need to know in order for the project to be fully beneficial?

E. *Community Activities*. Are project activities happening in the community as planned? Are the community members responding positively to the project?

F. *Support Services*. Are the necessary services outside the community functioning and available?

PROJECT CONTINUATION

G. *Local Organization*. Are the local people organized so they can and will manage and control the project themselves?

H. *Local Participation in Project Decision-Making*. Do local residents have anything to say about project decisions?

I. *Adequacy of Mechanisms for Mobilizing Resources*. Can local resources be collected, accounted for and used in the project for the benefit of the local contributors?

BENEFIT GROWTH

J. *Adoption of Recommended Practices*. Are local people doing things differently, for their benefit, since the project began?

K. *Individual or Household Resource Commitment*. Are local people contributing anything to the project?

L. *New Activities Beyond Project*. Are local people beginning to think of and do other things to improve their lives?

PROJECT REACH

M. *Total Communities*. How many communities will benefit from the project?

N. *Total Population*. What is the estimated total population of all the communities benefiting from the project?

ADDITIONAL INFORMATION

O. *Other*. What other project information is noteworthy?

Adapted from Donald Miller, "Project
Tracking System," MAP International,
1980, pp. 2, 12a-f. (REF. 2)

Periodic impact evaluation requires another form of reporting. Based on its own management procedures and resource levels, each PVO needs to develop a strategy of organizing information on its impact. The issue-oriented approach to impact evaluation advocated in this Sourcebook makes this a highly challenging activity. It is not limited to just reporting on achievement of previously planned objectives. Rather, it is an effort to sum up the evidence — so that the various audiences involved can learn from project achievements and failures.

Exhibit II-J

The Management of Impact Evaluation

There are a number of ways a PVO whose projects are relatively small, highly dispersed, and numerous can organize an impact evaluation. A few were suggested during our workshop series:

- Sampling of project sites. When coupled with rotation, this can assure program coverage over an extended period of time.
- Triage. Project sites are selected on the basis of need. Monitoring data can suggest which ones can benefit from an impact evaluation, leaving the more successful ones, or those evidently floundering aside.
- Intentional selection of areas that are either successes or failures is another approach, as lessons can be derived from all projects. The choice is dependent upon what an agency wants to know.
- Tiered. An information system can be structured so that each site has the detail it requires to make appropriate changes, while more generalized information would flow to other levels for coordination and learning.
- Periodic case studies can be used to complement ongoing monitoring, and substitute for other forms of impact evaluation.

from discussion paper: "Impact
Evaluation in Perspective," *Wingspread
Conference Report*, 1982, p. 15. (REF. 2)

As Chapter Four of this section suggests, to accomplish our desired evaluation goals, we will borrow from a number of different evaluation persuasions. The CIPP model (see "Decision Making Evaluation," page 70) offers an excellent guide for organizing evidence into a report. This approach suggests that all evaluative reporting include these factors:

CONTEXT — a summing up of the advances and the blockages the project implementor (e.g., community) experiences in trying to progress; whether or not they relate to the project's specific objectives.

INPUTS — an accurate measurement of time and material resources invested in the project.

PROCESS — a summary of evidence about what was done and how well it was done.

PRODUCT — evidence concerning the results of the project, planned and unplanned.

Let us now return to our design of a hypothetical evaluation to see how this format might be used.

In preparing a report on our project, the evaluator might use the following Table of Contents:

   I. Introduction
      A. Program Objectives and Evaluation Plan
      B. Community Context
      C. Program Inputs

  II. Issues for Evaluation (in order of importance)
      A. Community Participation
          1. Process for selecting leadership
          2. Results and Conclusion
      B. Participatory Training
          1. Instructional Process
          2. Results and Conclusion
      C. Nutritional Status
          1. Gardening Program
          2. Results and Conclusion
      D. Program Decisions
          1. Process of decision making
          2. Results and Conclusions

 III. Summary and Recommendations

This example suggests one way to apply the CIPP framework. Obviously, there are many variations on this theme. You must guarantee that the basic pieces of the evaluation are put together in an effective manner for the intended audience.

Why Did It Happen?

An answer to the question "What Happened?" leads naturally to our next question "Why did it happen?". It is not, however, idle to emphasize the importance of focusing on the "Why." In most cases, understanding what happened in a specific project is not sufficient to answer "Why did the project succeed (or fail)?" If evaluation is to become the learning tool we desire, then an additional effort is needed.

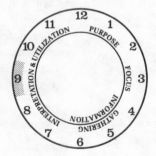

There are two steps to consider when addressing "Why": look for the Big Pattern and Compare and Compose.

The Big Pattern

One can expect too much from evaluation. Many evaluators fail because they make pompous claims that are simply not relevant to real life situations. These claims may be backed by elaborate designs, a mountain of statistics, and sophisticated findings. Unfortunately, the definitive study seldom is. Therefore, it is preferable that PVO evaluations strive to *show patterns* rather than prove an hypothesis. They should limit themselves to illuminating *key issues* rather than contributing to a new theory about development. Building from this more modest base, we believe PVOs can make an important contribution to the field.

Compare and Compose

In our framework for evaluation, this step is essential to attribute convincingly project effects. In other words, if we can compare the results of a number of independently conducted evaluations, then we will be able to compose more reliable answers to our "why" question. If several evaluations identify community involvement in the planning of a nutrition project as a key factor to success, this conclusion becomes more convincing to our audiences.

Within a single agency, comparisons can be built into an evaluation system by including some of the same issues in every evaluation. An example might be the relationship of community leadership to participation. To identify Big Patterns another technique is to compare evaluations in a particular sector, such as primary health care. Well prepared comparisons will reveal patterns impossible to identify in any one evaluation.

To increase the reliability of PVO evalution results, there must be a sustained effort by the community to pool information and undertake joint analysis. In our workshops, three means of achieving this objective were identified:

- Contracted studies and forums of PVO staff to share independently conducted evaluations that have been organized around a particular issue or sectoral interest.

- *Exchange of staff* among agencies at various points in the evaluation process, such as data collection or interpretation.

- Joint field study and interpretation of results of programs conducted by a group of agencies.

What Lessons Did We Learn?

Once we have broached the question of why something happened, our openness to learning is complete. We seek lessons, articulate statements that facilitate the transfer of benefits from one experience to another. However, our values inevitably influence the lessons we perceive. It is reasonable to assume that most lessons simply reinforce existing values, especially those stemming from deeply held beliefs. So why go through the effort?

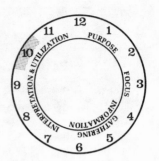

As stated in Section I, PVOs usually approach their work from a heavily value-laden position. Beliefs about peace and justice, the priority of helping children, or the importance of an individual's participation in society will not change because of an evaluation. Evaluation is better viewed as a means to modify habits or practices more susceptible to change, so that we can effectively serve the people we assist. Over time these modifications will test values and lead to significant changes in policies once thought immutable. Seldom, however, will these changes occur as a result of one particular program evaluation.

Therefore, we stress evaluation lessons more as a means of organizational growth and gradual education. Each evaluation audience may derive its own lessons. In particular, the community, which has the most at stake, may come up with lessons that are highly significant to the PVO. Any statement about lessons ideally comes from the interaction between people within and those outside the particular PVO. Each organization must consider the best means of achieving this goal.

What Will We Do Differently?

In Chapter Six of this Section, we consider further the issue of evaluation utilization. The process by which someone makes a decision is elusive, seldom easy to define. One way to begin to consider it is to ask what else might have been done. In this way, evaluation is an opening of options. One full revolution of the Evaluation Clock, a framework for systematic evaluation, is a means to realize the benefits of evaluation. A donor official, a PVO manager and a community leader all stand to profit from this quest.

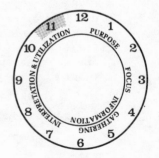

Exhibit II-K

A PVO Experience: American Friends Service Committee

AFSC went through an extensive learning experience as a result of its involvement in Tin Aicha, Africa, a project to benefit nomads affected by the Sahelian drought. Their experience is a rich example of how one agency articulated the lessons derived from field evaluation.

The AFSC worked in Tin Aicha between 1975 and 1980. During this period, field representatives provided regular reporting on the project. On two occasions, once three years into the project and again after its conclusion, AFSC contracted outside evaluators from the region to conduct some in-depth assessments of the project. They mostly used interviews and observation to gather information.

Realizing the significance of the experience and the rich evaluative material available, the AFSC African staff organized a four step review:
1) They gathered all documents concerning the original planning of the project as well as the evaluation reports from field staff and evaluators. This material was shared with a four-person subcommittee of the AFSC Africa Panel. (This panel consisted of fifteen persons with experience and expertise in Africa who helped guide program policy.)

2)After reading the material, a brainstorming session involving the AFSC international director, the Africa staff, and the sub-committee assessed the wider implications of the project for the organization.

3) From minutes of the session, the staff suggested some lessons learned. At a second meeting the same group refined the final statement of nine lessons.

4) This statement was reported to the full Africa Panel which endorsed it as a useful guide for AFSC planners.

The nine lessons were:

Lesson 1. A continued presence in an area through short-term projects and seminars builds up the knowledge and trust essential to the successful planning and initial execution of long term development projects. Even such associations cannot produce all of the key information needed; however, and programs must be planned flexibly and with the faith that they can be adjusted to respond to the real needs that arise as the programs proceed.

Lesson 2. Rehabilitation of a population following a crisis that includes natural disaster should take into account the human factors exacerbating the crisis, to avoid its repetition.

Lesson 3. The design of a development project should arise from experience in the field. The AFSC could not have planned Tin Aicha from Philadelphia before the project's inception.

(Continues)

Lesson 4. In a development project, the population must be allowed and encouraged to make its own decisions, once its decision-making structures are established and adequate information is available to it. Indigenous authorities must also be respected and supported.

Lesson 5. Goals for development projects will probably always be different from the different participants involved; even so, overlapping or generally consistent objectives can result in a successful project; for the outsider, openness and consistency in regard to motivation and aims is a strength for the project as a whole.

Lesson 6. A totally destitute population cannot become self sustaining without massive intervention, even at the risk of perpetuating excessive dependence. A delicate balance must be struck between self-reliance and adequate levels of technical and material assistance over time.

Lesson 7. To have a chance for permanent survival, an integrated development project for a given population requires eventual integration into local structures, after the pattern of other such settlements.

Lesson 8. A project that cannot be precisely duplicated may still contain valuable replicable aspects and have a significant multiplier effect.

Lesson 9. Even the most desperate of dispossessed people retain extraordinary strength, adaptability, and ingenuity. Outside assistance must be designed in full awareness of that fact and be provided in ways that call it forth rather than impede its realization.

American Friends Service Committee,
Tin Aicha Nomad Village, Philadelphia:
AFSC, 1982, pp. 125-32. (REF. 2)

CHAPTER FOUR
THE PRIMARY PERSUASIONS

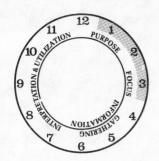

A Word of Caution

We have made bold to look at evaluation literature, to enter its eddies and swirls, and attempt to derive meaning for ourselves. This part of the Sourcebook does not originate from direct PVO experience. In our examination of the evaluation field we have found a welter of diverse opinions and conflicting arguments, too often a splitting of hairs more commonly associated with the discourse of philosophers and theologians.

These differences not only cover issues concerning what is appropriate evaluation practice, but they also include marked differences over the very terms of classification.

These practices are generally labelled "models" or "strategies," but never in the strict sense. More aptly, they should be called PERSUASIONS to which various evaluators adhere at different times.

We have carefully reviewed the extensive literature of the evaluation field and organized it into five primary persuasions. These categories are not definitive, they are intended to be most useful for PVOs. We present these five persuasions because they can help PVO staff:

1. Acquire a better sense of what is happening in the field of evaluation;
2. Understand more fully the possibilities open to us, beyond traditional models;
3. Encourage us to be creative;
4. Provide a correlation between our own experiences and ideas about evaluation and those of social scientists who have written on the subject.

The five persuasions contain the most important elements in evaluation. They emerged, historically, as responses to each other. Each is a corrective to a previous approach; yet, they are not necessarily mutually exclusive. A simple summary of and guide to the five persuasions follows:

The Persuasion	Major Purpose	Typical Focus Questions	Methodology
Goal-Based	Assessing achievement of goals and objectives.	Were the goals achieved? Efficiently? Were they the right goals?	Pre- and Post-testing; often quantitative; experimental designs.
Decision Making	Providing information.	Is the project effective? Should it continue, terminate, be modified? How?	Assess range of options related to project context, inputs, process, and product. Develop decision-makers' consensus on value.
Goal-Free	Assessing full range of project efforts.	What are *all* outcomes, intended or unintended? What is their value?	Independent determination of needs and standards to judge project worth. Quantitative and qualitative techniques uncover results.
Expert Judgment	Use of human beings as evaluation instruments and judges.	How does an outside professional rate this project?	Critical review based on experience, informal surveying, and subjective insights.
Naturalistic	Understanding project processes.	What is happening in the project? What does it look like to different people? How does it respond to their various concerns?	Inductive discovery using qualitative methods, open ended interviewing, participant observation, and case studies.

While reading this section, keep in mind the following recommendations:

1. These persuasions may be superceded in years to come. There are also other approaches which we have not included, such as systems analysis and the adversary approach, that may more adequately serve a particular need. Sources that discuss other persuasions are listed in the annotated bibliography. They have been chosen as points of reference.

2. The persuasions are not mutually exclusive. There is a great deal of difference between evaluation theory and practice, just as there is between development theory and practice. In practice, differing perspectives can be combined to strengthen an evaluation.

3. At the end of this chapter there are case study examples of evaluations from PVO experiences that illustrate these persuasions.

4. Our final recommendation is this: Borrow from each of these persuasions within the framework we have described to achieve the most satisfactory evaluation design. Above all, do not let yourself be boxed in by dogmatists. Evaluations do not have to focus exclusively on goal achievement, nor should naturalistic inquiry ignore previously established objectives. It is the blending of persuasions that offers the most creative approach to effective evaluation.

The Persuasion: Goal-Based Evaluation

DESCRIPTION: The goal-based evaluation embodies the classic strategies of evaluation research and is best known to the general public. It aims to determine whether a program has achieved its goals, and usually employs an experimental or quasi-experimental design model.

In its most basic form, the goal-based evaluation includes the following steps:

1. Determine the goals and objectives of the program;

2. Translate them into measurable indicators;

3. Collect data on the indicators for those involved in the program;

4. Compare the two groups of data in terms of the goals and objectives established for the program.

Goal-based evaluation also involves what is called a PROJECT IMPACT MODEL. According to Rossi and Freeman (1982) this model "takes the form of a statement about the expected relationships between program and its goal; it sets forth the strategy for closing the gap between the goal set during the planning process and the existing behavior or condition" (p. 62). It includes the set of hypotheses that underlie program planning and implementation. The best known application is the "logical framework" approach used by the Agency for International Development. The impact approach can also be used to answer other, related questions, including (1) were these the right goals and objectives for the program, considering the needs, resources, and participants? (2) were resources used efficiently in achieving the goals? and (3) did the achievement of these goals result in something of value?

In its most rigorous formulation, goal-based evaluation requires the random assignment of participants to either the project or the control group. Because assigning people to control groups is rarely possible in social service work (we would say impossible in ours!), other methods for developing control groups have been created. These groups match participants and non-participants in relevant aspects. Statistical techniques are employed to hold constant the differences between participants and non-participants. Established measures, such as published test norms, are sometimes used. Reflexive controls, commonly called pre- and post-tests, involve participants who are tested against specific indicators before, during and upon completion of the project. This is the underlying approach to the collection of baseline data, a process which PVOs have undertaken with varying success for some time.

PROS: Goal-based evaluations relate directly to the questions of accomplishment and causality. They aim to pinpoint achievements in concrete terms and relate them, as precisely as possible, to the project's intervention. Not surprisingly, they carry with them an aura of objectivity. Therefore, they are much desired by funding sources who seek clear cut demonstrations of the effectiveness of their financial support. An emphasis on quantification and measurement is most appropriate for projects with very tangible results, i.e., increases in agricultural production, income, and nutritional standards.

CONS: The goal-based approach has been criticized as an artificial evaluation approach. Human development programs do not easily conform to the strict standards of a traditional scientific experiment. The effort to determine causality has two requirements: First, the rigorous control over numerous variables so as to isolate what are called "confounding factors" — i.e., the real, context-laden environment we work in; second, the reduction of these to a self-selected, quantifiable few. This manipulation of reality poses serious problems for professional evaluators, let alone PVO practitioners. That which lends itself to measurement may not be of greatest significant to PVOs and project participants. "Before" and "after" research designs assume that program contexts undergo little or no change during the period of study. This is rarely true in our experience. Finally, an exclusive focus on questions of goals and objectives may leave other important issues unanswered. Stakeholders may find the final study results of little or no use.

CONCLUSION: Despite these drawbacks, a goal-based approach has its place in PVO programming. We need to know about the measurable outcomes of our work — for ourselves, our project participants, and our donors. The key to the effective use of the goal-based approach is to realize its limitations. A too rigorous adherence to the approach can be counterproductive. The elements of the Evaluation Clock suggest that achieving stated project goals and objectives are part of our audiences' concerns, but there often are other, even more pressing, ones.

It is best to consider the goal-based strategy in concert with others. Obtain qualitative and quantitative information about goal achievement. You should be prepared to adopt elements from different experimental designs or seek other alternatives to match the reality of your work. A multi-element design not only provides more insights than a singular approach, but the use of various approaches can help verify assertions pertaining to causality. The more varied the lines of evidence we use, the more persuasive our findings are likely to be.

REFERENCES:

Agency for International Development. *Evaluation Handbook*, 4th printing. September 1976.

Rossi, Peter H. and Freeman, Howard E. *Evaluation: A Systematic Approach*. 2d edition. Beverly Hills, CA: Sage Publications, 1982 (REF. 3)

Weiss, Carol H. *Evaluation Research: Methods of Assessing Program Effectiveness*. Englewood Cliffs, NJ: Prentice-Hall, Inc. 1972 (REF. 4)

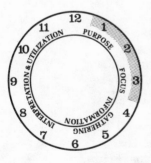

The Persuasion: Decision-Making Evaluation

DESCRIPTION: Whereas goal-based evaluation takes goals and objectives as the primary focus, the decision-making approach focuses upon decisions as the main element in developing an evaluation design. Daniel L. Stufflebeam and Marvin C. Alkin are major proponents of this persuasion.

In theory, this approach is the simplest: evaluation supplies information on decisions to be made. In practice, however, it is far more complicated, since decision-making is a complex process. The input of multiple actors with different viewpoints and values is a factor that must be considered in any important decision.

The CIPP Model. Stufflebeam's CIPP (Context, Input, Process, Product) model (1971) presents an heroic attempt to deal with different, even conflicting, realities by developing a system of classifications that identifies (1) the *process* of decision making (2) the *settings* in which it occurs (3) the *decision models* most appropriate for each setting (4) the basic *types of decision* which are made, and (5) the *types of evaluation* which serve each best. Four decision types are generated by crossing in a matrix of end-means and intended-actual dimensions. The four resulting decision types are matched to four inter-related evaluation types. The following chart summarizes this structure:

Decision Type	Purpose	Evaluation Type	Description
Planning (intended ends)	To determine objectives	Context	Macro-analytic and system oriented; defines the relevant environment, describes desired and actual conditions, identifies unmet needs and unused opportunities, and diagnoses problems; compares actual and intended system performance on continuous basis.
Structuring (intended means)	To design programs, projects, and procedures	Input	Provides information to determine resource utilization by assessing agency capabilities, strategies for achieving program goals, and designs for implementing a selected strategy; decisions based on input evaluation often result in project proposals.
Implementing (actual means)	To utilize, control and refine procedures	Process	Detects procedural design defects in implementation; provides information for program decisions; maintains a record of the procedure as it occurs; directed toward project improvement.
Recycling (actual ends)	To judge and react to attainments	Product	Measurements and interprets attainments, not only at the end of project cycle, but as often as necessary.

This framework expands the goal-oriented notion of evaluation, which is retained as Product Evaluation. It adds preproject assessment and process concerns. It also stresses overarching study and analysis of organizational context. For PVOs, examples of context include continuous monitoring of First and Third World realities, the latest professional thinking on development theory and practice, and specific institutional considerations pertaining to agency performance. As Stufflebeam concludes: "...evaluation is the process of delineating, obtaining, and providing useful information for judging decision alternatives." (Stufflebeam 1971, p. 40.)

Evaluators who use the decision-making approach are expected to work closely with the decision maker(s). Together, they will determine which alternatives are under consideration and which criteria will be applied in reaching the final decision. This can be fraught with difficulties when there are multiple decision makers, especially when they hold different viewpoints or values. We regularly face such situations when doing joint programs in cross-cultural settings.

Role of Evaluators. There are differing opinions as to the role of evaluators. Stufflebeam (1971) recommends that evaluators "help identify the different value positions..., the criteria that emerge from the different value positions..., and the alternatives to achieve the different goals...." The evaluator should present not only a realistic assessment of success for each alternative, but likely compromises where conflicting goals are involved (p. 91).

Edwards, Guttentag, and Snapper (1975) recommend the use of a unique technique to evaluate outcomes. The various actors or groups are taken through a carefully laid out process of self-examination. They define key issues (decisions), identify needs to be evaluated (plans, strategies, products, etc.), develop a list of values or criteria, rank them in order of importance and weight them relative to each other, and, finally, decide how to act (pp. 148-151). The technique is useful for planning an evaluation as well as for establishing a "consensus" as to the value of the evaluation. Where groups disagree, the process is worked out separately for each group. The same evaluation data is given to each group and they, individually, judge it in accordance with their specific values. The groups can then relate better to each other, having a clearer idea of areas of agreement and disagreement.

Agreement in some areas diminishes disagreements in others. The "consensus" technique is ideal for developing evaluations that respond to the demands of many stakeholders.

PROS: One obvious advantage of this approach is its focus on decision makers as the cornerstone of an evaluation design. Data is gathered about a broad range of questions that can assist decision makers with specific decision alternatives. This approach can also "frame the decision context," as Alkin calls it, by responding to knowledge uncertainties which cloud activities and options, thereby greatly enhancing the use of evaluation materials. Techniques that attempt to get at the heart of value conflicts result in more meaningful studies. They can also contribute to a shared understanding of a project's overall worth, as well as develop greater commitment to its success.

CONS: The principal difficulty with this model is that it is based on assumptions which tend to view decision making as an essentially rational process. In fact, decisions are often political in nature. They respond less to "hard" evidence than the pressure of relevant forces. They are also affected by ideology, tradition, and human emotion. Operational decision makers are not always easy to identify: As Guba and Lincoln (1981) note, "in complex organizations or loosely coupled organizations decisions appear to 'bubble up' rather than to be made at some particular time and place" (p. 16).

CONCLUSION: Decision-making evaluation is useful to PVOs who generally cannot afford to use a more expensive research design. An overemphasis on decision making can be counterproductive, when it is, for example, performed primarily to satisfy a donor's decision on funding. Once again, a balance is in order. The CIPP framework is a useful organizing tool because it outlines a broader scope of evaluation. The CIPP framework can make explicit the values underlying decision making, which can be invaluable to a PVO. Therefore, as our framework suggests, decisions are an important part of your focus when undertaking an evaluation. Borrow from this model when appropriate.

REFERENCES:

Alkin, Marion C. "Evaluation Theory Development" in Carol H. Weiss, ed., *Evaluating Action Programs: Readings in Social Action and Education.* Boston: Allyn and Bacon, Inc., 1972, pp. 105-117. (REF 4)

Edwards, Ward, Guttentag, Marcia and Snapper, Kurt. "A Decision-Theoretic Approach to Evaluation Research," in E. L. Struening and M. Guttentag, eds., *Handbook of Evaluation Research*, Vol. 1. Beverly Hills: Sage Publications, 1975, pp. 139-181. (REF 4)

Steele, Sara. "Use of Evaluation in Resource Management Decisions." University of Wisconsin-Extension, 1981. Mimeographed. (REF 5)

Stufflebeam, Daniel L. et al. *Educational Evaluation and Decision Making.* Itasca: F. E. Peacock Publishers, Inc., 1971. (REF 4)

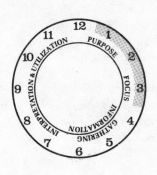

The Persuasion: Goal-Free Evaluation

DESCRIPTION: Goal-free evaluation is one of the most intriguing approaches to evaluation. It was originally proposed by Michael Scriven, a well-known evaluator who first coined the terms FORMATIVE and SUMMATIVE. Reflecting on his experience in evaluating educational products, Scriven reports: "...I became increasingly uneasy about the separation of goals and side-effects. After all, we weren't there to evaluate goals as such....All that should be concerning us, surely, was determining exactly what effects this product had (or most likely had), and evaluating those, whether or not they were intended." (Scriven, 1972, p. 1).

The Goal-free strategy involves certain unusual elements:

1. The evaluator—assumed to be an outsider—is not provided any information regarding program goals or objectives. This is done to eliminate the bias that knowledge of goals can create. The evaluator is thus forced to uncover all outcomes, as he or she is not predetermined to look in a particular direction.

2. To judge worth, the evaluator employs external standards against which to measure or assess project outcomes. These standards might be derived from the funding agency or from those commonly accepted within a given field. They could be derived from a profile of demonstrated need in a particular instance. To the extent the project satisfies these needs, it is to be judged as having worth.

3. Compared to other evaluation models, the evaluator's contact with project staff is minimal. There is no initial project orientation nor other substantive discussions with staff. This decreases the possibility of bias that occurs by coming to appreciate them as people. As Scriven notes, "How can all these nice intelligent people who show their good taste by asking after my health and work so interestedly and even, in formative situations, by selecting and paying me to do the evaluation possibly not be doing something worthwhile?" (1976, p. 136). Instead, the evaluator must focus on the viewpoint of project participants. In this way, he will be more likely to see results, not rhetoric.

PROS: The greatest advantage of this approach is that, by ignoring project goals as the focus of inquiry, it elevates the project participants' perspective to a much higher level of prominence. Scriven believes that goals and objectives are often overstated and couched in the fashionable language of the day for fundraising purposes. Proposal writing "assumes that a gallant try at Everest will be perceived more

favorably than successful mounting of molehills." (Scriven, 1972, p. 2).
For the evaluator to consider seriously such goals is often only
confusing.

Because most projects fall short of their intended goals, it is best to
study what actually has happened in terms of those directly affected.
Cooperation by those implementing projects is also reduced, and a
more objective view is possible.

CONS: This strategy is intended for use by outside evaluators. A PVO
could conceivably do an internal, goal-free evaluation only if the
organization were large enough. Program staff, other than those involved in or knowledgeable about the project, might serve in the role of
independent consultants. But it would be difficult to ensure the objectivity required.

A more serious difficulty arises when determining the standards
against which to assess identified effects. If needs assessment is used,
the question is, Whose needs are being considered? The goal-free
evaluator is not supposed to simply adopt those of the implementing
agency. Nor can he or she simply substitute a subjective rendering of
needs. One alternative is to use a survey of a similar group, which can
be very hard to find. Another way to set standards is to make a logical
extrapolation. What can a program of this magnitude, implemented
under these circumstances, be expected to produce? Whatever choice
is made, the evaluator must be able to justify the standards used as the
instrument of judgment.

This approach also requires the evaluator to uncover all possible project effects. Scriven says that the evaluator must act like a hunter "setting snares" where his experience tells him animals might come. The
evaluator must be well acquainted with the field in order to know
where to identify unexpected effects.

Scriven suggests that one of the best ways to conduct a goal-free
evaluation is in tandem with a goal-based approach. He says that two
different teams should work on the project. In this way, a full range of
insights would be generated, with each evaluation serving as a double-
check on the other. We doubt PVOs can consider this idea because of
the cost factors involved.

CONCLUSION: The most important lesson to draw is that PVOs must not
become too goal oriented. They should not overlook other significant
program results not originally envisioned within the evaluation
framework. There is also an important benefit in emphasizing the com-

munity perspective in our projects rather than simply measuring results. Some experimentation with the goal-free approach might be just what voluntary agencies need, especially where a PVO wants an unbiased view of the impact of an important program.

REFERENCES:

House, Ernest R. and Hogben, Donald. "Setting Speculative Snares," *SRIS Quarterly* (now *CEDR*), Vol. 6 (1973) No. 1, pp. 11, 13.

Irwine, Jane F. "Goal-Free Evaluation: Philosophical and Ethical Aspects of Michael Scriven's Model," *CEDR Quarterly*, Vol. 12, No. 3, Fall 1979, pp. 11-14.

Scriven, Michael. "Pros and Cons about Goal-free Evaluation," with comments by Daniel Stufflebeam, Marvin C. Alkin, W. James Popham, and George F. Kneller, in *Evaluation Comment*, Vol. 3 (1972) No. 4. (REF 4)

_____."Goal-Free Evaluation" in Ernest R. House, ed., *School Evaluation: The Politics and Process.* Berkely: McCutchan Publishing Corporation, 1973, pp. 319-28. (REF 4)

_____."Evaluation Bias and its Control," in Gene V. Glass, *Evaluation Review Annual,* Vol. 1. Beverly Hills: Sage Publications, 1976, pp. 119-39. (REF 4)

The Persuasion: Expert Judgement as Evaluation

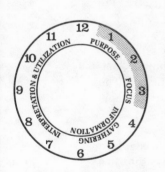

DESCRIPTION: A number of variations fall under the classification of expert judgment. Among these are the **ACCREDITATION APPROACH**, based on school certification methods, and the **ART CRITICISM** concept proposed by Elliot W. Eisner. In addition Rossi and Freeman consider expert judgment a form of "shadow controls," a category devised to cover what they consider less scientific and, to their minds, less reliable forms of evaluation.

These strategies are linked by the utilization of human judgment as the organizing principle. Key to each is the presence of an individual or team of evaluators who possess credibility due to their knowledge of and experience in a particular field. Less emphasis is placed on rigorous data collection procedures and more on the critical abilities of the chosen evaluator(s). The evaluators interpret information based on their own experience rather than use traditional techniques replicable by others. The methods employed include interviews, observations, and document reviews, but these are undertaken more casually than in other structured approaches.

Under the accreditation model, an evaluation team visits a project site and reviews pertinent materials. After careful review, a judgment about the project's operations and value is presented. The Eisner model (1979) uses the metaphors of art connoisseurship and criticism in striking contrast to scientific terms most commonly used in evaluation research. Because these models relate to situations seldom encountered by PVOs, those wanting further information should look to the references at the end of this discussion.

While it is doubtful that PVOs have had direct exposure to evaluators operating as connoisseurs and critics, it is certain that we have faced the type described by Rossi and Freeman: "a well-known expert or experts in a relevant field. . . hired as a consultant and sent to visit the site of a program to examine closely its works and to write a report summarizing experiences and assessments." The worth of such an evaluator depends upon his or her mastery of the discipline involved, knowledge of evaluation in the field, and effectiveness in communication. It also depends upon the substantive nature of the project itself. "In a field where knowledge of how to achieve a particular outcome is quite advanced," Rossi and Freeman add, "an expert's appraisal may be very accurate. If little is known about an area . . ., an expert's judgment may not be worth more than that of any other person." (p. 259)

PROS: A knowledgeable judge is a highly flexible and creative evaluator. Such a figure can provide insightful analysis, literary description, and rich, experience-based guidance to project staff and participants. His or her qualitative comments can add more depth to quantitative data. The use of indigenous evaluators offers the possibility of a more context-laden, culturally accurate review than is possible with outside experts. Finally, certification of quality by a prestigious evaluator can boost program credibility among donors.

Expert judgment is highly responsive to time constraints. While it can be undertaken over a long period of time, it can also be accomplished in fairly short order and is characteristically used for what are known as "quick and dirty" evaluations. Well-focused questions and schedules are essential for the success of this strategy.

As a complement to internal evaluation systems, the external evaluator can promote greater objectivity regarding project operations. Specialists can assist PVO practitioners and participants to be more aware of the latest advances in the field, and how these can be applied to community-based activities.

CONS: The use of expert judgment is more subjective and, hence, generally less valid than other, more "scientific," approaches. The validity of an evaluator's conclusions can, nevertheless, be tested. One can examine how the evidence fits together, as in a legal case, and determine whether what is reported actually existed. More importantly, the test of an expert's evaluation depends upon how much the program's overall vision is expanded as a result. Whether these tests of methodological adequacy are sufficient depend on the attitudes of the stakeholders and the purpose of the evaluation.

This approach depends heavily on the competence and credibility of the individual evaluator. Finding the right person to fit the situation is often a difficult and time-consuming task. When short-term site observations are undertaken, there is the possibility that the project has been "dressed up" for the occasion. As Rossi and Freeman note, ". . . one can expect the state of a project at the time of an announced visit to be better than at other periods, in ways ranging from neatness and cleanliness of the headquarters to possibly well-rehearsed laudatory statements from participants." (1982, p. 260).

The most serious deficit of the approach is its non-participatory character. Expert judgment rests strictly on the perceptions and wisdom of the evaluator or evaluation team. While they draw on interviews with staff, beneficiaries, and knowledgeable outsiders, this input is neither collected nor reported in as structured a way as in other approaches.

CONCLUSION: The use of expert judgment remains a valid evaluation approach. Done well, it can provide a fresh perspective on an often too familiar situation. The specialist's insights to particular problems can be illuminating to those caught up in day-to-day responsibilities. PVOs should implement this approach within the framework described in this Sourcebook, and, whenever possible, couple it with other more participatory evaluation efforts to validate findings.

REFERENCES:

Eisner, Elliot W. *The Educational Imagination: Or the Design and Evaluation of School Programs.* New York: MacMillan Publishing Company, Inc., 1979. (REF 4)

Rossi, Peter H. and Freeman, Howard E. *Evaluation: A Systematic Approach,* 2d ed. Beverly Hills: Sage Publications, 1982. (REF 3)

The Persuasion: Naturalistic Evaluation

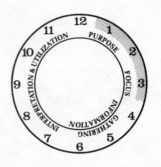

This persuasion represents the "newest wave" among evaluation professionals and includes such models as the responsive approach of Robert Stake, the illuminative method of Malcolm Parlett and David Hamilton, and the transactional form of Robert M. Rippey. In strong contrast to the goal-based approaches which take the "harder" scientific perspective as their own, naturalistic evaluation draws its inspiration from the "softer" science of anthropology and from disciplines as different as journalism. This shift in choice of paradigm opens the door to methodological innovation.

Fundamental to naturalistic evaluation is an emphasis on the pluralism in values and viewpoints which characterize each program setting, and a consequent belief that there is rarely one truth which all can accept. Rather than attempting an "objective" verification of goals and objectives, the naturalistic evaluator seeks to respond to a wider range of issues and concerns held by stakeholders, and in the process illuminate their multiple perspectives and possible conflicts. While information and, sometimes, judgments may be provided on goal accomplishments, as well as on a host of other matters, it is never assumed that a definitive balance-sheet of pluses and minuses will be the result. Rather, a naturalistic evaluation hopes to offer credible, confirmable information to project stakeholders that fits their various needs, and can serve as a point of reference for their respective actions and decisions.

The ultimate goal is an holistic understanding of program operations. To achieve this, the naturalistic evaluator does not attempt to manipulate the research setting through the establishment of an experimental design. Instead, he or she acts more like an anthropologist or investigative reporter, using an inductive approach to data collection and interpretation. The evaluator is less interested in testing the causal linkages of impact models, and more in drawing patterns, themes and categories from the reality itself.

The evaluator's approach is initially exploratory and open-ended. He or she develops a close interaction with the people involved in the project process. The methods employed are primarily qualitative in nature. Emphasis is placed on observation, especially participant observation, an unstructured interviewing of key informants, and on a scrupulous review of the historical documentation. There is an explicit attempt to understand the meanings of events as those involved perceive them, and to represent participants in their own terms and language.

The Products. The products of naturalistic evaluation include detailed descriptions of situations, events, people, interactions, and observed behaviors and direct quotations from people about their experiences, thoughts, beliefs and attitudes.

This qualitative data is presented to the audience in various forms, often far removed from the conventional research-reporting style. Robert Stake says that "the responsive approach is an attempt to respond to the natural ways in which people assimilate information and arrive at understanding." (1975, p. 23) Like ethnography, naturalistic reporting styles aim to provide the audience with a vicarious experience of what the program is like. These reports can be long or short. They include what Stake calls portrayals: a five minute script, a log, or a scrap book. "A long portayal may require several media: narrative, maps and graphs, taped conversations, photographs, even audience role-playing. The ingredients which best convey the sense of the program to a particular audience are chosen by the evaluator." (1975, pp. 23-24)

Most closely associated with this form of evaluation is the CASE STUDY, an extended narrative which provides a descriptive, readable picture of a person or program. The case study is presented either chronologically or thematically, and it makes accessible to the reader all the information required for a full understanding of the entity studied. Case studies are rich in detail and coherent representations of diverse views and complex situations. Ernest R. House notes that "everything from the personalities of the participants to the views of persons far removed from the program can be portrayed. This leads to power and utility of the information." (1980, pp. 244-245) The writing style tends to be more informal than in conventional reports, using everyday language, and much quotation, illustration, and even allusion and metaphor. The result is a vivid document of the inner workings of a program that can help the audience extend their experience and increase their understanding of the type of process depicted in the narrative.

A Focus on Process. Besides being process-oriented when it looks at projects and programs, naturalistic evaluation tends to be process-oriented in its own implementation as well. More traditional evaluation approaches tend to be what Stake calls "preordinate." The design is set at the beginning of the evaluation and implemented according to the pre-specified plan. Research-type reports are provided at agreed-upon intervals, often only at the conclusion of the study.

In contrast, the design of a naturalistic evaluation is emergent. That is, it evolves throughout the period of the evaluation itself in response to the needs of the stakeholders and to the issues as they develop. Feedback from evaluator to audience is provided on a continuous basis, often informally. In transactional evaluation, the evaluator becomes part of the operating system as much as possible, providing information to the program participants as needed. He uncovers sources of conflict in a program and aids the proponents and opponents to develop and implement evaluation plans which will help to resolve their differences and improve program performance.

PROS: Because naturalistic evaluation orients itself more towards understanding and discovery, it is highly attractive to PVO practioners as a mechanism for learning. In our projects, it is difficult to ascribe causality both because of the small size of our input and the collaborative nature of our endeavors. On the other hand, we are involved in efforts which provide real opportunities for illuminating the nature of participatory processes, a subject of great interest to the development community. Case studies and other "portrayals" can serve as an important mechanism for self-study and community learning, if conducted on a systematic basis.

A well-documented case study is one of the most powerful mechanisms in evaluation for communicating information. Written in everyday language, it can serve the needs of a wide variety of audiences, including the private constituencies of voluntary agencies. House comments that, if credible to the audience, the case study "has the potential for being persuasive, accurate, coherent, and just in representation of diverse views in complex situations." (1980, p. 247). In the cross-cultural situations in which we operate, a model which can incorporate multiple perspectives and values in its analysis has much to recommend it.

Finally, naturalistic strategies are harmonious with participatory development activities. They respect the project milieu, do not attempt to manipulate it experimentally, and approach people and situations openly. Responsive to stakeholders' concerns, they can be especially sensitive to beneficiary issues. The methods employed for qualitative data gathering can be less obtrusive than many quantitative procedures. And finally, their imperative to communicate in ways the audience understands means that evaluation data will not end up just in the hands of First World parties to the project. The innovative portrayals proposed by Robert Stake suggest interesting possibilities for reporting at the community level.

CONS: Naturalistic evaluation is less well suited to proving cause and effect than some other strategies. While questions of goal attainment can certainly be dealt with in a responsive approach, there is some trade-off in measurement precision that may not suit donor requirements. For those who have been oriented to the scientific view of evaluation and who expect definitive judgments rendered in accordance with traditional standards of validity, reliability and objectivity, (and this includes many in the PVO world), the somewhat more subjective style of naturalistic evaluation may not satisfy. Naturalistic evaluators are developing their own tests of rigor: Guba and Lincoln (1980), for example, have suggested concepts such as credibility, fittingness, auditability, and confirmability as appropriate counterparts to experimental standards. But an educational process may be required before more conservative audiences are willing to accept goal-based and naturalistic evaluations as equals.

While case studies have notable merits, they are not useful in all situations. As House argues, "Case studies are always long and involved. One does not have the time to read one in preparation for every decision. There are some efficiency trade-offs...." Further, "Writing a good case study is a difficult job and only certain people have the talent for doing it. It looks easy, just as writing a novel looks easy, and many are tempted by it who would not be attracted to other approaches. Unfortunately, the lack of methodological guides, strictures, and procedures often leads to poor quality work. And, a bad case study is bad indeed..." (1980, pp. 264-247)

Just as special skill is required for the preparation of case studies, it is also needed for uncovering the qualitative data out of which they are composed. Participant observation, key informant interviewing, and content analysis may appear easier on the surface than the construction of scales, questionnaires and other objective tests. But each involves procedures that must be followed. Experience in utilizing them as well as great sensitivity are also essential if results are to be unbiased. Further, practitioners must verify facts and assertions drawn from one form of data by cross-checking them with data drawn from other sources or discovered using different methods in order to assure the validity of what is said. Few PVO practitioners possess such skills or experience.

CONCLUSION: Naturalistic evaluation is worth the effort! The Evaluation Clock described in this Sourcebook draws substantially on the precepts of naturalistic inquiry. Using the clock requires a mastery of at least the basics of the naturalistic approach.

We believe that with some training and outside assistance PVO practitioners can master the required skills of observation, interviewing and content analysis, especially because, in PVOs, these are normal activities. This does not mean that PVOs should totally adopt the naturalistic or any other evaluation approach. Rather, we view this persuasion as valuable because it expands our range of options, giving us a creative opportunity we should not miss.

REFERENCES:

Guba, Egon C. and Lincoln, Yvonne S. *Effective Evaluation: Improving the Usefulness of Evaluation Results through Responsive and Naturalistic Approaches.* San Francisco: Jossey-Bass Publishers, 1981. (REF 3)

House, Ernest R. *Evaluations with Validity.* Beverly Hills: Sage Publications, 1980. (REF 4)

Parlett, Malcolm and Hamilton, David. "Evaluation as Illumination: A New Approach to the Study of Innovatory Programs." In *Evaluation Studies Review Annual*, Vol. 1. Edited by Gene U. Glass, pp. 140-157. Beverly Hills: Sage Publications. (REF 4)

Patton, Michael Q. *Qualitative Evaluation Methods.* Beverly Hills: Sage Publications. 1980. (REF 3)

Rippey, Robert M. ed. *Studies in Transactional Evaluation.* Berkely: McCutchan Publishing Corp., 1973. (REF 4)

Stake, Robert E. *Evaluating the Arts in Education: A Responsive Approach.* Columbus: Charles E. Merrill, 1975. (REF 4)

PVO Experiences: Case Examples

These four case studies represent a sampling of PVO evaluation experiences. They represent a useful cross-section illustrating the relevance of the primary persuasions described earlier in this Sourcebook. We are grateful to the following agencies for providing the examples:

Heifer Project International

Institute for International Development, Inc.

Lutheran World Relief

Overseas Education Fund

(Continues)

A PVO EXPERIENCE: HEIFER PROJECT INTERNATIONAL

Heifer Project International (HPI) implemented a series of field tests, which together provide evaluative studies of a significant cross-section of the HPI program. One such field test focused on HPI's program in the Philippines, a collaboration with a local implementing agency. The purposes of the field test were:

- "To field test the evaluation design, especially with regard to livestock production and local participation indicators.

- "To obtain a body of information which will identify the strengths and problem areas of the program in order to facilitate planning and decision-making....

"The methodology employed in this field study consists of four general stages: Preparation, Field Survey, Data Analysis and Presentation, and Post Evaluation Review and Planning. Three of these stages are completed with the submission of the (formal) report. The final stage is to be achieved by the three-day planning workshop discussed as a Recommendation."

Although the approach used went beyond the measurement of goal achievement, it was important for HPI to gather as much quantitative information as possible concerning their primary input, which is livestock. Therefore, HPI followed these steps in gathering information:

1) Organized a team of two HPI staff and an animal scientist to lead the field survey in collaboration with the local PVO.

2) The team trained local staff to implement the survey. A sample of project sites were chosen, taking into account geographical distribution, type and species involved.

3) The teams used an interview guide for obtaining general information and a questionnaire to collect specific production data over a one week period. All the teams met for preliminary analysis afterwards. The tabulation of production data was done by computer in the United States.

Using the preliminary evidence, the team discussed their analysis with the local collaborating agency. They then prepared a report of findings and concerns designed to serve as the basis for a joint planning workshop to make further goals and objectives more explicit.

The HPI example illustrates how a goal-oriented approach, implemented largely by PVO staff using both quantitative and qualitative evidence, constitutes an effective evaluation approach. Summing up, the HPI report points out, "In the evaluation of objectives and goals we cannot count only on statistics, but also must make value judgments regarding quality, attitudes and relationships."

Quotes from *Evaluation Field Test IV*
prepared by Armin Schmidt,
HPI Evaluation Director, February, 1981.
(REF. 2)

A PVO EXPERIENCE: INSTITUTE FOR
INTERNATIONAL DEVELOPMENT, INC.

The Institute for International Development, Inc. (IIDI) needed to make some strategic decisions caused in part by the implementation of an AID matching grant. To facilitate the evaluation, they obtained the help of outside consultants "familiar with PVOs and expert in strategic evaluation."

The purpose of the evaluation was to decide how their minimum operations should be modified. In order to accomplish the evaluation, information gathering was divided into three segments: strategic, strategic and operational, and operational. The methods used consisted of:

1) Intensive "question-and-answer sessions" between the consultants and IIDI leadership.
2) Open-ended interviews of stakeholders (e.g., board-members, sponsors, other PVO executives, overseas collaborators and experts in enterprise development).
3) A detailed questionnaire for field staff describing project activities.
4) Examination of project records.

As they gathered information, the evaluators discussed it regularly with the executive leadership. The process was a noteworthy example of continuous interpretation and utilization. Its product was described by IIDI in the following terms:

> "It is truly a self-evaluation, one which has been educational both as to the facts of our situation and a way of thinking about them. While we have used an outside firm to assist us, it has not played the judgmental role frequently associated with outside evaluations. Rather, their key roles have been:
>
> • To help us develop the insights only a fresh perspective — and a systematic, but flexible process — can provide.
> • To "keep us honest," i.e., to press the uncomfortable but important points we might otherwise miss, as well as confirm the pleasant ones we enjoy discussing.
> • To provide us with staff support (including drafting this report), a service in short supply at any time but especially useful when adding a major activity such as this one to our usual tasks.

This assessment deals as much with strategic issues as operational ones. For example, it answers the deceptively simple question, What "business" are we in? in addition to examining our success in meeting project objectives.

It is a document aimed at influencing our own behavior. For it combines evaluation with planning, and it presents objectives for the future as well as comments on the past and the present. It is a "motion picture" rather than a "snapshot." We will be using the guidance sketched in the following pages to know, manage and market IIDI better."

> Quotes from *IIDI: A Strategic (Self) Evaluation*
> prepared with Stan Druben and Ricci Associates,
> Fall, 1980. (REF. 2)

A PVO EXPERIENCE: LUTHERAN WORLD RELIEF

As the first in a three-part examination of their world-wide program, Lutheran World Relief (LWR) recently conducted an evaluation which involved contracting two outside experts as evaluators. The purpose of this effort was to satisfy a major donor's need for impact assessment and to provide LWR leadership with important information for a review of their program policies.

The evaluators prepared the following description of the methodology used in Niger, Africa:

> The evaluators, one a social scientist (anthropologist) and one a technical scientist (forester/engineer) conducted open ended interviews together and separately. They interviewed LWR staff (American and Nigerian), Nigerian government field agents and officials, project personnel, and local residents, both those involved and those not yet involved in the projects. They kept in mind the total information required but each took special care to cover his/her field of expertise. Each interviewer compiled daily field notes. From their combined notes they completed the data collection document, discussing each point and either reaching a consensus or noting various aspects presented by the projects.
>
> Finally, the evaluators worked directly with the stated LWR development strategy guideline program objectives and the ecologic guidelines. They added one column for significance in relation to size of area gardened or number of people affected, etc., and a column for intrinsic value in relation to the priority needs of the populaton. The evaluators made a chart upon which projects received high, medium or low ratings for each point. From this chart it is evident how each project ranked on each of 24 criteria.
>
> For the purposes of the end-of-project and mid-term evaluations each project was described as to its history and context, its current status, its impacts and potentials, lessons which had been learned, and recommendations for LWR.
>
> For the purposes of policy evaluation, the evaluators examined each of the stated objectives pointing out not only how well they had been met, but the fact that all the objectives cannot be met equally well in all projects in all environments. Some criteria are more relevant at certain levels of development than others.

The LWR experience applies the principles of expert judgment. It demonstrates the use of tools — naturalistic inquiry, open-ended interviews, and observation — within the approach. Stated goals, both at the level of the agency and the specific project, provide the standards for judgments.

Quote from "Evaluation of Lutheran World Relief Projects—Niger" prepared by Marilyn W. Hoskins and Fred R. Weber, Virginia Tech, February, 1982.

A PVO EXPERIENCE: OVERSEAS EDUCATION FUND

The Overseas Education Fund (OEF) has employed a participatory project evaluation system over the last two years with noteworthy success. The approach, described on page 55, involves three components: monthly evaluation meetings, a mid-point evaluation and a final evaluation. Recently, the OEF completed a mid-point evaluation, whose purpose is to measure the effectiveness of a small enterprise development project implemented in collaboration with a women's organization in Morocco.

OEF hired an independent consultant in the U.S. to coordinate the work. The OEF allocated a total of ten days in-country to go through the evaluation system's three stages: design, data collection and analysis:

Stage 1: Design Workshop. The consultant and the evaluation team met for a full day Design Workshop. The team included OEF's project director and project coordinator, a project assistant from the local women's organization, and the president and secretary of the recently formed cooperative of project participants. Most of the time was spent reviewing the three project objectives and the activities included under each objective. The discussion logically led to the selection of a number of priority issues for attention.

Stage 2: Data Collection. The Design Workshop planned a number of meetings (visits and interviews) that were conducted during the Data Collection phase. The plan was not followed exactly because a key decision-maker was not available to attend meetings. However, for the most part it was carried out according to schedule.

The information gathered included: figures on doll production to date; the attitudes of pilot project participants and of the community towards the project; identification of the women involved in the literacy course; and problems in project management and administration. The evaluator held meetings, reviewed documents, and gathered information which was introduced into the data analysis stage as appropriate.

Stage 3: Data Analysis Workshop. This workshop took place in two successive mornings. Each team member presented the data she had gathered. The team then analyzed findings on two levels: the community pilot projects and the local women's organization. The issues addressed included management of the project, participants' attitudes toward the activities, the future of the cooperative and the economic viability of the doll production and beekeeping ventures. Each issue produced specific recommendations.

The evaluation, then, begins with a distinct goal-oriented approach modified by a focus on issues of current concern to all the principle stakeholders. The team participates in the major evaluation steps (12:00 to 6:00 on our Evaluation Clock), using diverse, often naturalistic methods to gather as much information as possible in a short time.

The critical lesson of the OEF experience is that participation of the key decision-makers in each step of an evaluation is both possible and desirable.

Adapted from the midpoint evaluation report, "Improvement of the Socio-Economic Conditions of Low-Income Women in Morocco," Overseas Education Fund, 1982.

CHAPTER FIVE

USEFUL TOOLS:
A POTPOURRI OF INFORMATION
GATHERING METHODS

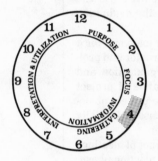

When it comes right down to it, being an evaluator is akin to being a detective. Both evaluators and detectives search out information, analyze what they find, and then reach conclusions based on their analyses. Sherlock Holmes had his magnifying glass...but what are the tools of the trade for those of us working in evaluation?

This section begins to answer that question by presenting sixteen different information gathering tools:

Action cards	Mapping
Analytical Frameworks	Measuring Nutritional Status
Community Meetings	Observation
Creative Expression	Photography
Diaries	Problem Stories
Farmer's Own Record	Questionnaire
Interviewing	Scales
Investigative Journalism	Unobtrusive Measures

These tools provide ways of putting into action some of the concepts of the earlier sections. They enable us to expand our repertoires. It is important, however, to keep in mind that the tools we use for collecting data often influence what we in fact collect.

The description of each tool has five parts: *Definition; How It's Used; Pros, Cons, and Other Issues; Participatory Applications;* and *For More Information.* The highlight on participation stems from PVOs' commitment to helping people to carry out development activities themselves, as emphasized throughout the Sourcebook.

The tools included here are intentionally diverse in scope. Some are geared to quantitative data and others to qualitative concerns. Some tools require reading and writing, others emphasize listening, and still others are mainly visual. Many of the tools are simple to create and use, while others are more complex and require considerable advance preparation.

It is important to remember that there is no direct match between the tools and the Primary Persuasions discussed in the previous chapter. For the most part, any of the tools can be adapted for use with any of the persuasions. For instance, an evaluation stressing a goal-based approach may encompass both quantitative and qualitative goals, so a method combining *scales, questionnaires, photography,* and *problem stories* might be appropriate. Likewise, a goal-free evaluation might make use of the same method, although with more open-ended items on the questionnaires and scales. The one exception in terms of matching persuasions and tools is probably naturalistic evaluation. Clearly, the less obtrusive tools, such as *observation, interviewing* and *unobtrusive measures* would be most appropriate in this case.

Generally, the key to effective selection and application of information gathering tools is the use of a number of tools in combination. Different tools by nature reveal different aspects of a project. For instance, *creative expression* may show individual feelings and opinions, whereas *action cards* certify certain verifiable tasks or accomplishments.

The use of a combination of tools also deals with the thorny issues of RELIABILITY and VALIDITY. These principles evolved from the scientific method and are two pillars of social science research. Basically, reliability means that *you can trust the consistency of a measure from one situation to the next,* validity deals with *the extent that a test measures what it is supposed to measure.* In evaluating PVO projects, it is usually not possible to find ready-made measures that are reliable and valid, while at the same time appropriate. Instead, project evaluators often are called on to create their own methods especially suited to the character of an individual project. Therefore, using a combination of tools provides a way to cross-check and confirm information gathered.

Another important key to effective information gathering is the use of PRE and POST tests. Traditionally, questionnaires have usually served as major sources of "before" and "after" data, but the less conventional tools in this section, such as *mapping,* are also adaptable for this purpose.

Information collection methods tend to be "catchy" or easily visible parts of the evaluation process, and therefore, decisions about data collection techniques are sometimes made early in the planning process. However, look back to the Evaluation Clock (p. 22), and note where this decision fits into our framework. The selection of an information gathering method should be coordinated with other basic decisions, namely, the kind of information needed, the evaluation approach(es) to be used, the level and complexity of the evaluation, the capabilities of the project beneficiaries, and the persons who will be involved in carrying out the evaluation process.

As you make those decisions, then, use this tools section as you would a spice rack! Be daring, and add a variety of new flavors to your evaluation. Or, if you're more a salt-and-pepper type, try one new seasoning at a time to add zest to your findings. In short, use this section as a resource for enriching what and how you evaluate.

Useful Tools: **Action Cards**

Definition:
Action cards provide a simple way of noting steps taken towards a goal and problems that were encountered. Blank index cards or brief, specifically designed forms (half sheets of paper with two or three questions) are used by individuals or groups to keep a running account of what they did, when, to reach their goal. Card entries can be short — a few words or sentences. The cards promote a sense of accomplishment and help identify critical project incidents or turning points.

How It's Used:
This evaluation tool was specifically designed for participant use. It is most appropriate for a self-help project, in which small groups or communities have decided to work together to accomplish a collective goal, such as starting a community child care center, forming a bee-keeping cooperative, or securing piped water for a village. Cards can be kept by all members of a group or by selected individuals. The events recorded can be major happenings only (e.g., rights secured to a parcel of land) or more detailed (e.g., meeting held with Mr. X, application presented to district office, etc.). Obviously, the more detailed approach gives a fuller picture of the project's activities.

Participants can use the cards at regularly scheduled meetings to assess their progress. By comparing the cards to a projected action plan or timeline, changes and needed revisions in the plan can be identified. The cards can also be shared with outside evaluators as a basis for discussion. An evaluator's questions and insights may help broaden a group's view of its activities. Also, the cards provide a concise record of outcomes.

Besides being useful for evaluation, the cards have a positive side effect: they reinforce goal-setting and planning skills amongst the participants. In using the cards, participants keep a longitudinal account of a specific set of activities and expand their capabilities for charting future activities.

Pros, Cons, Other Issues:
PROS: • Specific, concrete, action (outcome) - oriented.
        • Easy to use.

CONS: • If used alone, can place too much emphasis on results and not enough on how they came about.
        • Requires some writing ability.

This approach assumes that participants are clear on a project's direction and are committed to its goals. Also, action cards need to be introduced early in a project in order to have maximum value for tracking activities.

Participatory Applications:
The way participants use action cards can involve them to greater or lesser degrees in project analysis and policy-making. On one end of the spectrum, participants might keep cards which would then be compiled and analyzed by an outside evaluator. On the other end, participants would be involved in determining what to record, how to analyze and use the data, and with whom to share it. The latter approach enables participants to be not only sources of data, but first users of the data as well.

Action cards are an easy-to-use, easy-to-introduce evaluation tool that can effectively be combined with other tools to comprise a project evaluation strategy. The cards create a mechanism for building community participation in evaluation throughout a project, not just at the midpoint or when a project ends.

For More Information:
No published references available. Original work developed by World Education, 210 Lincoln Street, Boston, MA 02111.

Useful Tools: **Analytical Frameworks**

Definition:
An analytical framework provides a conceptual model for organizing and simplifying a complex process or situation. Typically, the frameworks are written outlines or graphic representations that are used as guides in examining the subject of the evaluation.

How It's Used:
Two analytical frameworks adaptable for PVO project evaluation are: **FORCE FIELD ANALYSIS** and **FUNCTIONAL ROLE ANALYSIS**.

Force field analysis can be used to look at any situation and determine the factors both contributing to and inhibiting desired change. For instance, a community women's group may have the goal of increasing their chicken production. With force field analysis, they would first brainstorm existing "supports" to chicken production (good stock, sanitary housing, proper feed), then brainstorm possible "constraints" (poor care of chicks, prevalence of disease). The idea behind force field analysis is that by maximizing positive forces and removing negative forces, goals can be reached. This framework is graphically represented as follows:

$$\text{existing situation} \underset{\uparrow\ \uparrow\ \uparrow}{\overset{\downarrow\ \downarrow\ \downarrow}{\rule{3cm}{0.4pt}}} \text{GOAL}$$

Functional role analysis is a useful overlay for examining social and task relationships, such as behavior and interaction in small groups. Group process outlines exist for this analysis and include criteria for effective "task" and "maintenance" behaviors.

Analytical frameworks can also be created for specific situations. For instance, a local PVO in Tanzania drew upon transactional analysis (see Jones & Jongeward) as a means to focus on respectful, participatory development and learning approaches. Their framework developed contrasted "parent-child relationships" and "adult-adult relationships" (see Vella).

Analytical frameworks work well with group discussion. The person presenting the framework needs to be able to explain it clearly and involve the group in applying it to their own situation. Following the discussion and analysis, recommendations and action plans can be developed.

Pros, Cons, Other Issues:
PROS: • Makes complexity manageable and changeable.
 • Often emphasizes specific skills; useful for behavior learning.
 • Leads directly to action steps.

CONS: • May be too abstract for some groups.
 • In some cases, may be too narrow in scope and exclude other important variables.

Participatory Applications:
Though analytical frameworks can be used by individuals, they are used most effectively for group discussion and analysis. To enable everyone to express their views — to get the fullest range of perspectives on an issue — small groups of four or five can meet, conduct analyses, and then report their ideas to the larger group. Next, the large group can work together to identify conclusions and "where to go from here," i.e., next steps.

Analytical frameworks are essentially participatory tools, as long as the participants clearly understand what the frameworks mean and how to use them. They are helpful in focusing discussion and in enabling groups to develop plans of action.

For More Information:
Jones, Muriel and Jongeward, Dorothy. *Born to Win.* Massachusetts: Addision-Wesley Publishing Co. Simple explanation and various applications of transactional analysis.
Pfeiffer, J. William and Jones, John E., eds. *A Handbook of Structured Experiences for Human Relations Training, Vols. 1-5.* LaJolla: University Associates, 7596 Eads Ave., Calif., 92037. Various group process frameworks.
Vella, Jane. *Learning to Listen.* Amherst: Center for International Education, 1980. Hills South, Univ. of Mass., 01003. Group process; transactional analysis applications to rural development.

Useful Tools: **Community Meetings**

Definition:
For the purposes of project evaluation, community meetings are a structured assembly for a large group of people that provide a forum for the following: a hearing on issues, a presentation of evaluation findings, a discussion of evaluation recommendations, and/or decision-making on plans of action.

Generally, community meetings are most appropriately used in combination with one of the other tools included in this section. Community meetings serve to open the evaluation process to more people and thus promote a greater sense of community involvement in project activities. The community meeting is basically a "presentation" tool, while the other methods are more "data collection" tools.

How It's Used:
Community meetings can utilize a wide range of formats: a visitor or expert panel presentation; community committee presentations; a fair or display (for instance, different kinds of wood burning stoves; or art work created by community members, see Creative Expression); a structured workshop; a presentation by community leaders; a debate; etc.

Whatever format is used, the process of a community meeting is essentially the same. First and foremost, community meetings must be well-planned and carefully structured because of the number of people involved. Community members ideally should be informed of what is to be presented at the meeting in advance, through a wall newspaper, flyers, home visits, radio, or whatever medium is available. When the meeting is held, its scope and purposes need to be made clear at the outset. Next, the presentation is given; it should be brief and geared to the level of those attending. Questions and discussion then follow. A good way to ensure that the discussion is not dominated by a few individuals and that there is time for everyone who wants to speak is to take a few questions from the floor and then break into small discussion groups. After a specified period of time, the large group can reconvene and hear reports from each of the small groups. To end the meeting, it is important to specify any decisions that have been made and any next steps planned. Since it is difficult for many people to agree on a course of action, suggestions can be referred to a community or project committee or to community leadership for their deliberation.

Community meetings can be held at "critical points" throughout the life a project, such as project identification and planning; mid-point review; and termination of outside technical assistance.

Pros, Cons, Other Issues:
PROS: • All-inclusive; all interested community members can attend.
       • Broadens community ownership of project.
       • When outside experts are involved, provides a "reality-base" for expert views and recommendations.

CONS: • Community conflicts may be manifested and go unresolved.
       • Difficulty in bringing closure to the meeting.

Participatory Applications:
Community committees involve a significant number of community members in meetings and encourage them to take more than a talking role.

The committees can perform the following tasks: collecting/analyzing data for presentation at a meeting; planning the structure of a meeting; coordinating logistics (space, publicity, etc.); making presentations at a meeting; following up on meeting recommendations by functioning as task forces. If a meeting is to be devoted primarily to an expert presentation, the preparation gives community members the feeling of having some part to play. Action task forces are excellent for translating evaluation findings into community commitments.

The composition of community committees will differ according to the interests of a particular community. Some may want representatives from major community groups; others may prefer voluntary participation.

For More Information:
Byram, Martin; Conchelos, Greg; Hall, Budd; Jackson, Ted; and Kidd, Ross.
"Emerging Rural Applications of Participatory Research." A Paper Prepared for Social Sciences Division, Unesco, Paris, 1978. Toronto: Participatory Research Project, International Council for Adult Education, 29 Prince Arthur Ave., Toronto, Ontario M5R 1B2, Canada. See esp. pp. 9-23.

Community Development Trust Fund. *Appropriate Technology for Grain Storage.*
New Haven: Community Development Trust Fund, 1977.

Community Meeting: Sample
In an AID-funded project in Ecuador, the Overseas Education Fund assisted the Tarqui Housing Community in establishing a multi-purpose community development cooperative. The initial activities of the cooperative included setting up a community market, community-based child care, and a training program for women entrepreneurs.

The mid-point project evaluation was carried out by an evaluation team, which included an expatriate consultant, project staff, and representatives of the cooperative. The team jointly planned what and how to evaluate. It gathered data and collectively analyzed the results.

As a handy way of compiling data, the team created a chart with three column headings: "Major Accomplishments," "Areas for Attention" (initially called "weaknesses), and "Recommendations for Action." The team found the chart helpful for structuring their discussion and for reaching consensus on what they had found and what needed to be done.

A few weeks after the team completed the chart, a meeting was called for community representatives to discuss the evaluation findings. The chart served as the focus for the meeting, and those present actively discussed the proposed recommendations. The outcome of the meeting was a chart that had been revised, particularly in the "Recommendations" column. Subsequently, the project's monthly reports and the final evaluation proved the commitment of community members to these recommendations. All the recommendations listed were acted upon.

One section of the market chart finalized at the community meeting follows:

Sample Market Chart

Major Accomplishments	Areas for Attention	Recommendations for Action
1. The coop and the project were successful in acquiring land, and an attractive, functional market has been constructed and began in March 1981.	1. The market is one year behind schedule due to legal delays in acquiring the land. As a result, the market has less time to work through its inevitable future management/marketing problems and achieve its financial projections.	1. By the end of the project cycle, coop and market employees should have access to outside expertise such as: a. a supermarket consultant; b. well known accounting firm to do annual audit; c. a bank for loans for equipment, etc.
2. Construction was low cost compared to similar buildings due in part to contributions in-kind from the provincial government.	2. The construction cost exceeded the original budget, because of inflation and the delay in securing necessary approvals.	2. No recommendations for action.
3. The coop leaders and some members feel a great responsibility to make the market a success and recognize that the credibility of the coop rests with the market.	3. A rather limited group of members has been active.	3. More members and residents should participate, e.g., make the landscaping job a big community event, not just a task.
4. There has been a high degree of participation from cooperative members in all aspects of planning, negotiating with the bureaucracy, and purchasing.	4. Apart from the market committee and weekend work groups for landscaping the area around the market, there has been little voluntary labor contributed by members. AID/OEF made all financial contributions.	4. In future projects, AID and OEF project planners should not be overly optimistic about using volunteer manual labor for construction in such projects, but might consider participation in other areas.
5. Community people are running the market, not outside experts.	5. There has been little training on supermarket management (note: such training is not available in Ecuador).	5. Staff should continue to seek useful manuals or training programs in supermarket management.
6. The Friday practice markets were successful in reducing prices.	6. The indigenous traveling vendors, who came to the community after plans for the market were underway, are losing business and will have to move to another town.	6. The project staff should consider unintended consequences of the project and look into the welfare of these vendors. (Continues)

Major Accomplishments	Areas for Attention	Recommendations for Action
7. The Tarqui Community is generally in favor of the market.	7. Many non-coop residents seem uninformed about the market or not to know about the details. Some publicity has been undertaken by the cooperative (except radio Tarqui broadcasts). However, some residents did not believe the market would become reality.	7. More publicity is needed to make people feel the market is theirs.
8. Coop leaders are concerned about the displacement of the local women with food stalls. Appropriate solutions were discussed and a relocation policy has been set.	8. Final details for the relocation for the local food vendors need to be worked out.	8. The cooperative must include the vendors in the discussion of relocation and reach a mutually satisfactory solution for their businesses.
9. Market has the potential for serving as a buyer and seller for local products.	9. No systematic search for local producers has been made so far as the market is a basically consumer cooperative, not yet part of the production/consumption cycle planned.	9. Review survey data on small businesses and seek local suppliers.

Useful Tools: **Creative Expression**

Definition:
Creative expression as an evaluation tool involves the use of art forms as a means for individuals and groups to represent their ideas and/or feelings. This method is very open-ended; it can generate data that is particularly rich for interpretation and contains many subtleties. Artistic forms that are commonly used include drawing, drama, role plays, music, found objects, and collages.

How It's Used:
With creative expression, it is important to choose an art form with which those participating in the evaluation are comfortable. In some cultures, for instance, folk dramas are a part of people's lives, and expressing reactions to a project through drama may be quite natural. After choosing the appropriate form, the individuals or group participating are usually given a question or theme to guide their work, such as, "How has the project affected the community?" or "Before the project/after the project." Basically, four kinds of guiding questions or themes can be used: 1) optimal (prescriptive: how participants would like something to be); 2) actual (descriptive: what they see happening in the present situation); 3) problem (descriptive/analytical: critical issues, why they exist, and what to do about them); and 4) comparative (how participants see two different periods of time, two different projects, etc.).

In evaluations with individuals or small groups as participants, the participants work on their creations and then present them to the full group for reflection and analysis. When groups work on one art form together (such as a collage), they stand back to look at and think about what they've created. In both cases — individuals or small groups — the creation(s) becomes a representation to "decode" and analyze, then draw conclusions and make plans for the future.

Here are some suggested art forms:

- Drawing: charts, maps, timelines, pictures, abstract free form, social interaction networks, cut-outs, diagrams
- Drama (usually longer than role plays): before and after stories, different perspectives on same issue through different characters; story of a problem
- Role play: critical incident, problem situation, role reversal, how to solve a problem

Pros, Cons, Other Issues:

PROS: • Literacy skills not required.

- Art works usually represent a wide range of views and mirror complexities.
- Process is fun and promotes interaction/discussion.

CONS: • Some participants may be inhibited in expressing themselves through art forms.

- Analysis and interpretation can be complex; hard to reach conclusions.
- Some funders may consider creative expression too "soft" an evaluation tool.

Participatory Applications:
Creative expression lends itself naturally to participation. The process of using an art form for evaluation is actually more like a workshop than the administration of an evaluation instrument. The evaluator serves as a facilitator, establishing the focus for the art form, then guiding the participants in creating, and finally posing questions to aid in analysis and drawing conclusions.

Whether the art works are created by individuals separately or individuals as a single group, all participants contribute to interpreting what has been created. Emphasizing this collective analysis and planning — making recommendations, revising a project implementation plan, modifying project goals — maximizes the participatory use of this tool. Collective analysis and planning takes time, but the time invested yields participants who share a sense of ownership and commitment to project activities and directions.

For More Information:

Kidd, Ross and Byram, Martin. *Popular Theatre.* Participatory Research Project, International Council for Adult Education, undated. 29 Prince Arthur Ave., Toronto, Ontario, Canada, M5R 1B2.

Laedza Batanani: Organizing Popular Theatre. Popular Theatre Committee, Institute of Adult Education, University College of Botswana, Private Bag 0022, Gaborone, Botswana.

Marino, Dian. *Drawing from Action for Action: Drawings and Discussion as a Popular Research Tool.* Participatory Research Project, International Council for Adult Education. Toronto: undated. (See "Kidd" above, for address.)

Russell, Robert. *The Fun Bus.* Amherst: Center for International Education, Hills South, Univ. of Mass., 1977. For community drama.

Vella, Jane. *Visual Aids for Nonformal Education.* Amherst: Center for International Education, Univ. of Mass., 1977.

Creative Expression: Sample

In Sri Lanka, the Overseas Education Fund worked with the Women's Bureau (Government of Sri Lanka) to expand the capabilities of rural development officers in working with rural women. The first phase of the-two year program included training in group building, mobilizing local resources, and specific income generation and health activities, such as pig raising and first aid. Phase two included initiating village level pilot projects with rural women.

As part of the end-of-project and final evaluation activities, a two-day workshop was held for the development officers to assess their experiences and plan continuing activities. One of the workshop activities involved the development officers in expressing their thoughts and feelings through drawing. A long sheet of brown paper was put up on the walls of the workshop room. Over ninety participants gathered along the paper and drew whatever each felt expressed the major accomplishments of the training. The drawings and accompanying phrases were extremely creative: a woman's face and blossoming flower (see above); ascending steps; a face changing from a frown to a smile; "systematic knowledge"; a rising sun/"awakening"; a flower breaking ground and growing; "cooperation."

When the project evaluator and staff presented their findings to representatives of the funding source, they used the development officers' drawings to convey the qualitative aspects of the project. The paper was put up in the funder's conference room before the meeting was to begin. That way, during the subsequent discussion about increases in income and changes in health practices, the representatives were surrounded by the very human context in which these outcomes took place.

Useful Tools: **Diaries**

Definition:
Diaries are records of events that occur over time. They record how the events happened, the problems that occurred, and peoples' feelings and thoughts about what transpired. Diaries can be kept by individuals, groups, or communities; they can focus on a narrow topic, such as rice planting and harvesting, or on wider aspects of community life, such as community development efforts.

Diaries are a unique source of data in that they record activities as well as personal reflections on those activities.

How It's Used:
Diaries need to be introduced early in the life of a project, and participants may require some training to use them effectively. It may be useful to review samples of other diaries. Participants may also want to meet after they've made a few entries to discuss what makes a valued entry and problems they may have encountered. Diaries can be kept in blank notebooks, or packets of forms, or even on cassette tapes for participants with minimal literacy skills. Guidelines should be set to determine what is to be included in the diaries and how often entries are to be made.

The data from diaries can be compiled in one of two ways. First, an outside evaluator can collect the diaries at specific times and review them. Second, participants themselves can meet to share their entries and discuss their themes and perceptions. The questions of who will have access to the diaries and how the information will be used should be determined from the outset. Some participants may be unwilling to present parts of their diaries to an outsider or even to another community member.

Diaries have been used creatively in some development programs. For instance, in Bolivia, farmers kept "technical agricultural diaries" to record how they carried out crop and livestock tasks (see Hatch, 1981). The information in these diaries was considered so valuable by agriculturalists that it is being compiled into a "people's textbook."

Thus, the diary material is useful for a number of purposes: tracking the life of project activities; identifying major turning points or problem areas; noting changes and accomplishments; getting a picture of individual satisfactions and dissatisfactions — even promoting learning among community members or between communities.

Pros, Cons, Other Issues:
PROS: • Combined focus both on project contents (what happens) and process (how it happens)
        • Creative — reinforces writing and analysis skills.
        • Enables participants to be the first users of the evaluation data.

CONS: • Generally, requires writing skill (though participants may dictate entries to school-age children or use a cassette tape instead of a notebook).
        • Generates a large amount of data, making compilation and analysis a challenge.

Participatory Applications:
Diaries are useful evaluation tools because participants control the data that is gathered, recorded and shared. Therefore, the approach described for using diaries is highly participatory. If trust is promoted among community members or between community members

and an outsider, the data from their diaries will often be more comprehensive than if it had been gathered through interviews or questionnaires.

Groups and communities can also keep diaries collectively. Individuals can make entries in turn, or groups can discuss together what to include. Such collective diaries, in addition to presenting a composite view of project activities, become a means of self-reflection for groups and contribute to building solidarity.

For More Information:

Hatch, John K. "Peasants Who Write a Textbook on Subsistence Farming: Report on the Bolivian Traditional Practices Project," *Rural Development Participation Review*, Winter 1981, Vol. 2, No. 2. Rural Development Committee, 170 Uris Hall, Cornell University, Ithaca, New York, 14853.

_____. "A Record Keeping System for Rural Households," Michigan State University Rural Development Series, Working Paper No. 9, 1980. (write: Dept. of Agricultural Economics, MSU, E. Lansing, MI 48823). Includes various "instruments," such as a gameboard for crop enterprise accounting. (REF. 5)

Diaries: Sample

On the next page is a chart to register costs and production which has been utilized by farmers, some illiterate, in Bolivia, Peru, Panama, Costa Rica and other countries. Farmers copy on to a board the grid depicted in the chart, and place a nail in each square. The farmer places a chip representing a unit of input for each category of production costs on the board during the appropriate phase of crop enterprise. A different chip is hung in the Harvested Production box for each unit collected. With a minimal outside assistance, this information allows the farmer to keep a running account of his most important activity, which can then be entered into a diary.

Diaries: Sample (continued)

Different categories of production costs incurred in growing the crop.

	FAMILY LABOR	HIRED HELP	ANIMALS	MACHINERY	IRRIGATION	SEED	FERTILIZER	INSECTICIDE	Harvested Production
LAND PREPARATION									
PLANTING									
CROP CULTIVATION									
HARVEST									

Adapted from:
John Hatch, "A Record-Keeping System for Rural Households."

Useful Tools: **Farmer's Own Record**

Definition:
Perhaps the ultimate level at which evaluation must occur is the individual. A farmer, for example, should be the final judge as to whether he/she should adopt a new technique. The best way for a farmer to decide is to test the new idea on a small portion of his/her land. By keeping records, the farmer can evaluate the merits of the new idea.

How It's Used:
There are a number of criteria which a farmer uses to determine whether or not to adopt a new practice. Included are the cost/benefit ratio, the amount of time and labor required, the availability of resources and desirability of product, and many more. Though these factors are often judged subjectively, some of them can and should be measured quantitatively.

A farm record can help a farmer keep track of input costs, total time spent on various operations, etc. These items can then be weighed against the difference in yield between the control plot (traditional practice) and the trial plot (new practice being tested). An objective evaluation then can be made.

Cost records are kept of amounts spent on seed, fertilizer, insecticide, tools, paid labor, etc. Amount of time spent on each operation can be recorded in hours, or more simply, in half-day units, i.e. mornings or afternoons spent doing an operation on that plot. Such a record is reproduced in the accompanying sample.

Pros, Cons, Other Issues:
PROS: • Farmers can keep records if they are literate enough to write numbers and have a knowledge of simple mathematics. They can thus add up the costs of inputs and compare them with the estimated value or actual sale of produce to determine net profit or loss.
  • Even illiterate farmers have been taught to keep records like those illustrated here. Farm records which use drawings, could be adapted for measuring other factors needed for individual-level evaluation.

Participatory Applications:
If one agrees that the ultimate "evaluators" are the individual beneficiaries, the concept of farmers being taught to measure and record their inputs and yields is basic to an agricultural development program.

The participatory approach to evaluation acknowledges the validity of people making their own decisions. If a farmer is taught how to measure and keep records, he/she can decide whether or not a technique being recommended by an extension agent will really be an improvement.

But this approach has an even greater potential. Not only can farmers be taught to evaluate an outside recommendation; farmers can test their own ideas and develop their own improved practices. This unleashes a revolutionary potential, with millions of inspired innovators experimenting and accelerating the development of agriculture!

For More Information:

Bunch, Roland. *Two Ears of Corn.* Oklahoma City: World Neighbors, 5116 North Portland Avenue, Oklahoma, 73112, 1983.

Hapgood, David, ed. *Policies for Promoting Agricultural Development.* Report of a Conference on Productivity and Innovation in Agriculture in the Under-Developed Countries. Center for International Studies, Massachusetts Institute of Technology, undated.

Harwood, Richard R. *Small Farm Development, Understanding and Improving Farming Systems in the Humid Tropics.* Boulder: Westview Press, 1979.

World Neighbors — 3 filmstrips: "Testing New Ideas" (Africa); "Let's Try It!" (Guatamala); "How to Test a New Idea" (Guatamala). (see "Bunch" above, for address.)

Farmer's Own Record: Sample

With very little training, even farmers who do not know how to read and write can be taught how to keep records of the time they spend in varous activities. By making one mark for every half-day spent doing specific jobs, Komian was able to compare the time he worked on his control plot with the time spent on his test plot.

An adaptation of this sort of record might be suitable for use with farmers in your project.

FARM RECORD	CONTROL PLOT	TEST PLOT
Preparing ground	IIII	IIII II
Planting	II	III
Weeding	IIII II	IIII
Spraying		
Harvesting	II	III

From:
World Neighbors filmstrip:
"Testing New Ideas"

Useful Tools: **Interviewing**

Definition:
The oldest and most respected manner of gathering information known to man is human conversation, or for our purposes - interviewing. The style of interviewing may range from informal and conversational to closed and quantitative. The objective in all cases is to provide a framework for respondents to express their understanding in their own words.

How It's Used:
For PVO practioners, interviewing simply requires the perfecting of a common task: talking to people. Doing it right, though, requires more than a casual approach. Including interviewing in evaluation is a must when one wants information that cannot be observed. We suggest four variations to structure interviews to collect information for an evaluation:

Preparation	Style	Purpose
1. Background infor- mation only	informal conversation	discovery
2. Interview guide	unstructured	open-ended probe
3. Standard questions	structured	open-ended verification
4. Questionnaire	limited responses	closed verification

The first three alternatives are primary means of gathering qualitative data, while the fourth is more quantitative. In all cases, interviewing should never be the sole means of gathering information. Rather, it should serve in corroboration with other evidence.

Analysis of interview data is painstaking, but rewarding. Recording interviews helps tremendously, but if that is too inconvenient, the interviewer must take detailed notes during and immediately after an interview. The evaluator should check the analysis with those closely involved in the observed situation, and then build a persuasive case, using generalizations that draw on specific points from the interviews. Tolerating ambiguities in most instances is a virtue.

Pros, Cons, Other Issues:
Interviewing provides the richest source of data in the shortest time. Its reliability is greater than any other form of information gathering from individuals because of the face-to-face interplay that occurs. Its principal drawback is frequently the cost. This factor should be weighed carefully against the value of the information. Also, interviewing is a skill that should not be taken for granted. Training, at least in the basics, is a must. One should consider the pros and cons of each style of evaluation:

1. *Informal conversational:* PROS: Discovers questions; builds well on observations, brings out deviations from usual responses. CONS: Hard to systematize and analyze; difficult to use different interviewers.
2. *Unstructured:* PROS: Keeps interview flexible, but easier to systematize information collection. CONS: Variations in questions posed affect responses.
3. *Structured:* PROS: Maintains comparability of interviews; easier to analyze responses. CONS: More restrained answers; restricts relevance of replies.
4. *Limited responses:* PROS: Quick interviews; possible to use various interviewers, produces quantifiable data. CONS: Impersonal; can distort responses; not useful for probing.

Participatory Applications:
Interviewing has obvious potential as a participatory technique. The community's involvement begins with the formulation of questions. A field worker can easily train community members to conduct interviews becuase it is a natural activity. Analyzing responses may require more assistance, but does not require technically sophisticated skills. Interviewing can be an excellent complement to community meetings, bringing out information people are unwilling to discuss in groups. Relating people's views in their own words can bring about effective communication of community concerns to others.

For More Information:
Dexter, T.A. *Elite and Specialized Interviewing.* Evanston: Northwestern University Press, 1970.
Guba, E.G. and Lincoln, Y.S. *Effective Evaluation.* San Francisco: Jossey-Bass Publishers, 1982. See especially chapter 7 on interviewing, observation and non-verbal cue interpretation. (REF 3)
Patton, M.Q. *Qualitative Evaluation Methods.* Beverly Hills: Sage Publications, 1980. (REF 3) Chapter 7 deals specifically with interviewing, but chapters 8 and 9 are also helpful on analysis of data.

Interviewing: Sample

World Education Reports in its October 1977 special issue on evaluation, describes a system which included the use of group leaders as interviewers developed for a family life education project. Regular and frequent home visits provided a continuous information feedback that detected changes in behavior and attitudes produced by the project. The group leaders perfected their own technique as the eight rules they developed demonstrate.

Group leaders discussed how they should behave when interviewing would-be learners. They must, they agreed, be "patient," understanding, goal–oriented, simple and accurate in expression, undemanding, unimposing, cooperative, respectful and "unbraggerating." Group leaders also agreed on what they must not do: "make a rude approach, despise and degrade the participant, repeat things too many times, confuse the participant, get angry or show any superiority that could instill inferiority complex on the part of the recipient." Eight rules were finally chosen:

1. Make the Interviewee comfortable.
2. Show more interest in the person than in the filling of forms.
3. Observe the interviewee and watch his or her facial expression during the interview.
4. Be aware that reading the sentences in the form does not convey the message fully. Your explanation of the message with the right interpretation is absolutely essential.
5. You are not investigating the interviewee but gathering information which is important to prepare yourself for class discussion.
6. The records need to be as readable as possible.
7. The group leader should interview participants, if possible, before they start class.
8. After finishing the interview, please submit the questionnaire to the office as soon as possible.

Techniques of Inverviewing
— *World Education Reports*
October 1977-updated September 1980, p. 8.

Interviewing: Sample

DO'S AND DON'TS FOR INTERVIEWERS

DO *give a clear statement of the purpose of the interview.* This will help legitimize your presence and questions and will put the respondent more at ease. He or she may want to know the purpose of the study, how he/she was selected, and if he/she can see the results.

DO *emphasize the confidentiality of the material.*

DO *ask if the respondent minds if you take notes.*

DO *record comments or remarks just as they are given.* The exact words people use to describe their feelings are important. If the comment is lengthy and you cannot write down every word, make notes that give the sense and the style of the comment. Use abbreviations that are understandable. Get specific comments, not vague, meaningless generalities like "I like it because it is good," or "because it is interesting," or "it's okay." Ask WHY in such cases.

DO *keep talking as you write.* Ask the second question as you record the response to the first. Start the respondent thinking about a question. Keep the pencil and interview guide as inconspicuous as possible. Keep eye contact with the respondent, and do the writing unobtrusively.

DO *focus the respondent's attention on the question.* If he wants to talk about something else, politely but firmly start him back to the questions. Smile and say, "That's interesting...now what would you say about this question?"

DO *get all the information you are asked to get.* That means, ask every question and record every answer — in the correct place. Check over the interview guide at the end of each interview before you leave the respondent's presence. Say, "Now, let's see if we've got everything," to allow you to look over each question to see that it is answered and the answer recorded correctly.

DO *watch for vague or qualified answers.* Vague answers may at first seem to answer the question, but really do not. Never accept a "depends" or "qualified" answer the first time it is offered as an answer to any question. Repondents will often use phrases such as "well, that depends," "yes, but...," "I really can see both sides of that question," etc. When you receive such answers, PROBE for a more complete answer.

DO *watch for ambiguous answers.* Recognize ambiguity when it occurs and probe as necessary.

DO *probe for response, if necessary.* Repeating the question is the basic method and the safest and most effective way or probing. Be sure you repeat only the question as stated in the interview guide.

DO *be flexible* as unexpected problems arise.

DON'T *offend the respondent in any way.*
DON'T offer comments which seem to place a value judgment on the respondent's answers.
DON'T let your tone betray your thoughts — Keep an even tone.
DON'T cut the person off in mid-answer, even if the answer doesn't seem completely relevant to the question.
Avoid superimposing your own view; try to draw the respondent out if the answer is unclear.

Prepared by Frederick B. Williams and
Mary M. Cate. *Project Evaluation Handbook*
Washington, D.C.: ACTION, 1982. (REF. 5)

Useful Tools: **Investigative Journalism**

Definition:
Investigative journalism is a method of inquiry used to expose a situation or condition inimical to the public interest. As an evaluation tool, investigative journalism is one of the new techniques developed at the Northwest Regional Educational Laboratory (Portland, Oregon). The Laboratory is carrying out a long-range project that emphasizes "metaphoric adaptation," which simply means using a discipline or field of activity not traditionally linked to evaluation as a way to gain new insights into a project. The project is based on the idea that dominant approaches to evaluation (i.e., social science methods) are inadequate for dealing with evaluation issues that are related to management, policy, value, and economics. It contends that new methods are needed to respond to expanded evaluation concerns. Thus, the aim is to broaden evaluation perspectives on ways of knowing and on how data is gathered and perceived.

How It's Used:
While the premise on which investigative journalism is based may not be appropriate for PVO evaluation, the processes can be useful for guiding open-ended inquiry.

Investigative journalism assumes that some wrong-doing or conflict of interest situation exists. It starts with a hunch, then sets out to prove the hunch is true. In PVO projects, conflict of interest circumstances may arise within a project or in relation to the local community. For instance, a local official may be tapping project funds for non-project purposes or determining who attends a particular training program. Usually, such situations are extremely difficult politically and must be handled in such a way that good PVO relations can be maintained with collaborating organizations. Or, a policy decision must be made to stop working with a particular organization or in a particular area. In general, journalists can afford to alienate the subject of their inquiry, whereas PVOs cannot.

In terms of processes, however, investigative journalism has much that is adaptable for PVO evaluation. This involves a series of steps: the hunch or hypothesis (for PVO projects, this could be related to a problem, such as limited participation, rather than to an assumption of wrong doing); exploration; and tracking. Different techniques support these steps. "Exploration" typically involves informal discussions, observation, and some document reviews. "Tracking" is much more rigorous; this step includes detailed study of written records to identify themes and connections, cross-checking of sources, and a key interview or interviews with those on whom the evaluation focuses. These techniques have been thoroughly developed through investigative journalism experience and interested PVO evaluators are encouraged to consult the sources in "For More Information" for complete guidelines and tips. Investigative journalism seems especially appropriate for monitoring or formative evaluation.

Pros, Cons, Other Issues:
PROS: • Provides a format for delving into critical problems or issues and for gaining a full understanding of their complexities.
       • Combines both quantitative and qualitative data; comprehensive.

CONS: • If used by an outside evaluator, may seem too much like a "detective investigation." If used by local team, may demand too much in terms of literacy and abstraction skills.
       • Can identify conflicts that may be beyond the scope of the project to resolve.

Participatory Applications:
An outside evaluator using investigative journalism techniques may be regarded by project participants with suspicion, so this tool may actually require participation in order to be used successfully in the field. At the same time, the techniques probably need to be simplified for participants and/or community members to be able to use them.

A participatory approach for carrying out evaluation like investigative journalism would involve a team of participants coordinated by an individual well-versed in the techniques, possibly an outside evaluator. The role of the coordinator would be to guide the team in planning, in developing needed skills, and in implementing the plan. The planning could be done in a workshop, structured according to the steps used by investigative journalists (hunch, exploration, and tracking). For each step, the evaluator would explain the kind of inquiry and techniques typically utilized, and participants themselves could identify similar techniques suitable to their own skills and context. For instance, rather than do extensive cross-checking of written references, participants might decide to cross-check many different individuals.

In a nutshell, a participant team uses an investigative journalism approach to determine a key area to examine in depth, define ways to find out and confirm information, carry out the investigative plan (meeting regularly to cross-check data and identify new leads), and finally reach conclusions. The coordinator enables the team to become detectives in their own situation.

For More Information:
Guba, Egon G. "Investigative Journalism." In *New Techniques for Evaluation*. Edited by Nick L. Smith. Beverly Hills: *Sage Publications*, 1981, pp. 167-262. (REF 3)

Nelson, David E. *"Investigative Journalism Methods in Educational Evaluation."* In Field Assessments of Innovative Evaluation Methods. Edited by Nick L. Smith. San Francisco: Jossey-Bass Publishers, 1982, pp. 53-81. (REF 3)

Note: The above publications also include articles on some of the other "new methods" for evaluation developed by the Northwest Regional Educational Laboratory in Portland, Oregon. These include adaptations of film criticism, philosophy, committee hearings, and watercolor painting.

Useful Tools: **Mapping**

Definition:
Mapping refers to making graphic representations of specific aspects of a community, i.e., social structure, communications networks, neighborhoods, historical development, and resources. It is a structured activity in which individuals or groups diagram a part of the context in which they are living. As an evaluation tool, mapping is especially useful for "before and after" reactions and for recording perceptions of project impact.

How It's Used:
Maps are fairly simple tools to create and use, as long as participants are able to make the connection between their milieu and some lines and figures drawn on a piece of paper. Many kinds of environments can be represented on maps — entire communities, organizations, households, coops, businesses, and small groups. Within these environments, many different kinds of structures and relationships can be considered, i.e., social relationships, economic structures, leadership, decision-making, resource utilization, etc.

Typically, maps are either linear, to demonstrate how something evolved, or holistic, showing an environment in its entirety.

To use mapping, the specific focus of the map must first be established. This focus and the instructions for creating a map then need to be clearly explained to participants. It is very helpful to have a sample from another community, because the idea of a map may be new to some. Maps can be drawn by individuals or by group members together and subsequently should be analyzed by the full group.

Maps tend to highlight critical elements of whatever is being considered, such as landmarks in the development of a group or community organization, or key problem areas in resource utilization and control. Participants should be encouraged to represent what they perceive as most important and not to worry about details.

Many segments of a population should participate so that a range of perspectives are represented.

Pros, Cons, Other Issues:
PROS: • Generates many different perspectives and provokes rich analysis.
      • Can lead to new discoveries.
      • Results in a graphic product that can be referred to in the future.
      • Promotes greater understanding in a group or community of different viewpoints.

CONS: • Sometimes complex, hard to interpret.
      • May be difficult for some groups to conceptualize.

Mapping of areas that can be sensitive, such as decision-making patterns or resource control, may produce strong differences of opinion within a group. The individual coordinating the evaluation needs to be skilled in facilitating discussion and in dealing with conflict.

Participatory Applications:
"Collective creation" and "collective analysis" are the ways to promote full participation in using mapping for evaluation. The more diverse the viewpoint of those who are involved in

making the map or maps, the broader the range of representations on the maps. Diversity will enrich the subsequent discussion and analysis.

Mapping of social, economic, and historical relationships is much more subjective than geographic mapping. In fact, this method is most effective with wide participation so that many perspectives are included.

Wide differences of opinion can also represent a challenge, particularly for arriving at conclusions and recommendations for the future. Following general discussion/analysis, participants may want to form a task force to review, summarize, and identify some directions from what has been said. These could then be presented at a later date to the larger group for consideration.

For More Information:
Marino, Dian. *Drawing from Action for Action: Drawing and Discussion as a Popular Research Tool.* Participatory Research Project, International Council for Adult Education, Toronto, undated. 29 Prince Arthur Ave., Toronto, Ontario, Canada, M5R, 1B2.
Participatory Research Project. *Participatory Research Handbook for Community Groups.* International Council for Adult Education, Toronto, undated. (Same address as above.)

Sample: Mapping

Historical Mapping...

This process has been used in different ways depending on the group and the problem. Basically it consists of re-presenting *past events* and linking them to *present* and sometimes *future* happenings. It is a way that problems which have been predominantly analyzed as *personal* can be put out for analysis at a *structural level.*

Way one: each person is asked to draw *their own map* of the development of the group, or project, or course, etc. Usually there is a great deal of diversity in structures, symbols, details and depth in these productions. For example, one map might be wholly *diagramatic*, while another drawing might look more *pictorial*, while another might read from *top to bottom.*

The next step is to cover a wall or floor with paper (taped together), so that a *collective map* can be constructed. It is probably a good idea to have everyone take a quick look at how their individual maps look and then begin with the person who has the most past dates or events. (This can either be done up by one drawer or by the group.) The collective map is usually richer than the individual ones. After the initial collective map is produced it can then be re-used to add layers of information which were only hinted at in the first production. This might call for home-work or added research.

There are many modifications to this process...Sometimes two groups will find themselves not working effectively together so they can both sit down and map out some of the history of the working relationships...this can result in making a new relationship to each other.

Individual mapping or collective mapping is a useful way to bring new people into a group as well as review a state of the art of the group's history.

Also the group can find out things about itself that weren't "common knowledge." New pieces are often added.

Adapted from Dian Marino. *Drawing from Action for Action: Drawings and Discussion as a Popular Research Tool.* Participatory Research Project: International Council for Adult Education, undated.

Useful Tools: **Measuring Nutritional Status**

Definition:

The basic goal of most development programs is an enhanced quality of life for the beneficiaries. Unquestionably, one of the most basic aspects of quality of life is the nutritional status of children. Consequently, knowing how a program has directly or indirectly affected the nutritional status of a community's children is an important element in the evaluation of almost any program.

Nutritionists use a wide range of measurements, but here we will focus only on those anthropometric measurements which can be used by field workers with minimum training.

How It's Used:

1. *Weight for age:* Commonly used on the "Road to Health Chart" developed by Dr. David Morley, monthly weighings of an individual child are recorded on a graph with current age as one axis. Results are compared with standards (i.e., Harvard) for classification (i.e., Gomez) into grades of malnutrition based on percentiles.
2. *Height for age:* Height versus age is compared with a standard (i.e., WHO) giving an indication of the duration of past malnutrition, or stunting.
3. *Weight for height:* When compared to reference, this measure can be used to classify children as a) normal, b) malnourished but not retarded, c) malnourished and retarded, or d) retarded but not presently malnourished.
4. *Weight for height for age:* This combination of measurements, arranged in tabular form, indicates categories of stunting and wasting.
5. *Arm Circumference:* In children between the ages of 1-5 years, the mid upper arm circumference does not vary much except as a consequence of nutrition. Over 13.5 cm. is considered normal; 12.5 cm - 13.5 cm is considered mild to moderate malnutrition; below 12.5 cm is severe malnutrition.

Pros, Cons, Other Issues:

1. *Weight for age:* PROS: Good indication of present status. When plotted on Morley's "Road to Health" chart, dynamic visual representation of child's progress is a good educational tool for mother. CONS: Requires scales. If not started early, determining correct age can present a problem.
2. *Height for age:* PROS: Indicates chronic malnutrition. CONS: Need for correct age can throw off accuracy when comparing with standard tables.
3. *Weight for height:* PROS: Eliminates need to know age. Gives an estimate of present or very recent nutritional status. CONS: Needs to be compared with standards.
4. *Weight for height for age:* PROS: Provides index of body build. CONS: Requires proper scales, standard tables, trained personnel.
5. *Arm circumference:* PROS: Very easy measurement, requiring little training; simple strip can be homemade. Age independent (roughly 1-5 age group). Suitable for rapid survey of present nutritional status in community. CONS: Not as useful as "Road to Health" chart for individual child.

Participatory Applications:

The Road to Health chart is now being used around the world in many programs where children under five years of age are weighed once a month. While gathered for weighing, mothers can participate in health and nutrition education classes. Village volunteers often do the weighing and teaching. The chart is good visual aid for helping a mother realize the need for good nutrition, sanitation, etc.

Taken once or twice a year (i.e., during the "hungry season" and after the harvest), arm circumference measurements provide data on current nutritional status of the community. Over time, these measurements serve as an evaluation tool to indicate change in nutritional status. Village volunteers, even school children, can take the measurements. Community health committees can understand the results and determine effectiveness of the program.

For More Information:

Jelliffe, D.B. *The Assessment of the Nutritional Status of the Community. Geneva:* World Health Organization, 1966.

Latham, M.C. *Human Nutrition in Tropical Africa.* Rome: Food and Agriculture Organization, 1979.

Morley, D. & M. Woodland. *See How They Grow.* London: MacMillan Press, 1979.

Waterlow, J.C. "Classification and Definition of Protein-calorie Malnutrition." *British Medical Journal,* Vol. 3, 1972, pp. 566-569.

World Health Organization. "Rapid Village Nutrition Survey Technique." Brazzaville: WHO, 1977.

Measuring Nutrition Status: Sample

A weighing/arm circumference control card
to be given to each participating child

Name of Child _____

(to be completed by Staff)

Village: _____

Date of Vaccination: _____ Type of Vaccination: _____

Arm Circumference (band in 3 colors)	Initial Weighing Date: Weight: Health Status: Other Observations:	2nd Weighing Date: Weight: Health Status: Other Observations:	3rd Weighing Date: Weight: Health Status: Other Observations:
Red	(Good nutritional status)		
Green	(Transitional Nutritional Status)		
Yellow	(Malnutrition)		

Adapted from Diane Hedgecock,
"Review of Health and Nutrition Sector:
Save the Children, Dori, Upper Volta,"
February, 1982.

Useful Tools: **Observation**

Definition:
"Seeing" and "listening" are the key words in defining observation. As an evaluation tool, observation means going to view the results of a project (a new well; erosion) or participating in a slice of project activities. Observation can be obtrusive (everyone knows why the evaluator is there) or unobtrusive (people are not told the real purpose of a visit). It can also be directed (structured by a list of questions, guidelines, etc.) or undirected (open-ended). Because observation is fairly simple and often a natural part of field evaluation approaches, it is often overlooked as a legitimate evaluation method.

How It's Used:
Observation for evaluation has its roots in one of the principal research methods of anthropology, "participant observation." The anthropologist actually lives with a community; watches, listens, and shares in daily activities; keeps extensive field notes; and draws conclusions about common patterns and themes. An anthropologist may focus on the culture of an entire community or on a specific aspect, such as parent-child relationships.

For project evaluation, the same general sequence of activities occurs but with two major exceptions. First, the evaluator(s) usually face time constraints related to the length of observation. Second, the observation is typically more a shared process in which a team of evaluators observes and jointly compiles their insights.

Before beginning an observation, it is important to agree on time and focus: How much time is adequate and available to spend at a particular site? What will be observed — will the observation be open-ended or guided by a specific framework? When these decisions are made, a practice session in observing may be helpful for less experienced team members. Next, the actual field observation takes place. Finally, the team meets to discuss their impressions and to draw conclusions. Sufficient time needs to be reserved for this critical last step.

Some ways of using observation for project evaluation include the following: visiting a site to observe concrete changes, such as production of new crops or construction of a new coop; visiting a number of homes to observe changes in sanitation procedures or purchase of consumer goods; attending a meeting to observe leadership and interaction patterns; spending a day at a health clinic to observe staff functioning; living in a village for a week — before and after a project — to observe any changes. Many more possibilities can be added to this list.

Pros, Cons, Other Issues:
PROS: • Easy to do, requires minimal preparation.
          • Tends to be holistic, taking many factors and influences into account.
          • Particularly with open-ended observation, effective in identifying unintended as well as intended project outcomes.

CONS: • Depends heavily on perceptiveness of observers and their own biases.
          • People may change their behavior if they know they are being observed.

Participatory Applications:
The major considerations for using observation in a participatory way are *who* is involved and what *roles* they play. As a means of focusing the widest range of "lenses" on whatever is being observed, both community members and outsiders should be included on the evalua-

tion team. Ideally, this team would jointly carry out all the steps in the observation process, from deciding what to observe to interpreting the significance of what is observed.

To involve even more community members, the team could present their conclusions and any recommendations in a community meeting (see "Community Meeting" description). This would enable community members to contribute to analyzing and charting the course of project activities, thus reinforcing the sense of community ownership.

Since observation is a subjective tool, broad participation ensures that a range of perspectives will be represented and increases the likelihood of accurate analysis.

For More Information:

Schatzman, Leonard and Strauss, Anselm L. *Field Research: Strategies for a Natural Sociology.* Clifton: Prentice-Hall, 1973.

Vella, Jane. "Listening," In *Learning to Listen*. Amherst: Center for International Education, 1979. Hills South, Univ. of Mass. 01003.

Williams, Thomas Rhys. *Field Methods in the Study of Culture*. New York: Holt, Rinehart and Winston, 1967.

Useful Tools: **Photography**

Definition:
Photography can vividly document project outcomes, project processes and activities, and project impact on participants and their communities. Photographs — still or moving — may be visual vignettes, portraits, or stories from people's environments and lives. Photographs are like mirrors of reality. Unlike many other evaluation tools, good photographs carry emotional as well as intellectual messages and may reveal aspects of a project not evoked in structured interviews or questionnaires.

How It's Used:
Photography for evaluation encompasses a wide variety of formats: still photographs of people, places, and things; collages; albums; photonovellas or comic books; socio-dramas (still or moving); films; videotapes; and slide presentations.

Basically, any of these forms of photography can be used either to *document* aspects of a project (e.g., "before" and "after," meetings, training programs, etc.) or to *stimulate analysis* related to interpreting project problems and impact.

The use of photos for analysis has been developed most fully by Brazilian educator Paulo Freire. Freire suggests that a visual image is a "code" for certain key issues and realities faced by participants. Through a questioning process stimulated by the photograph, participants gain insights into their situations and how they might deal with them. For the purposes of evaluation, this process can involve participants in solving specific project problems (such as management difficulties) or in determining ways a project can be more effective in dealing with a community problem (such as lack of water). The following questions can guide the photographic analysis:
- What do you see happening here?
- Why does it happen?
- Does this happen in your situation?
- If it does, what problems does it cause?
- What can we together do about it?

Regardless of how the photos are used, an issue of utmost importance is the photo's "truthfulness." Truthfulness is really a function of individual viewpoint and interpretation. Thus it should be clear who has taken or chosen a photo, and efforts should be made to represent differing views (staff, participants, other community members, etc.).

Pros, Cons, Other Issues:
PROS: • Presents a "slice" of participants' real environment.
      • Evokes wide range of reactions.

CONS: • Equipment and supplies may be costly for resources available.
      • Cultural constraints or political censorship may limit what can be photographed and by whom.

Participatory Applications:
Since photography provides true-to-life images of project participants' realities and does not require literacy, it is especially well-suited for use by them.

Participants can be involved in actually taking pictures as well as interpreting them. Some initial and follow-up training is likely to be necessary in using cameras and other equipment. Then a plan can be developed for using photography over the life of a project. For example, photos may be taken at certain intervals and key photos discussed. Or, participants may decide to keep an album of project activities and events. In communities where participants have actually utilized photographic technology themselves, participants have gotten deeply involved in project activities and seem to have increased their problem-solving abilities. Using a camera can give a villager a new sense of power and help him/her to see old realities in new ways.

If photographs are taken by project staff or an outside evaluator, participants still have an important role to play in deciding which photographs present the most accurate depiction of the project or community and in analyzing the photos' meanings. Structured group discussions provide the best format for involving participants in these processes.

For More Information:
Barndt, Deborah. "Visual Interventions in a Participatory Research Process: How a Camera can Enrich Interaction and Inquiry." Participatory Research Project, International Council for Adult Education, July, 1977. 29 Prince Arthur Ave., Toronto, Canada, M5R 1B2. July 1977.
Becker, Howard S. "Do Photographs Tell the Truth?" In *Qualitative and Quantitative Methods in Evaluation Research*, Vol. 1, Sage Research Progress Series in Evaluation. Beverly Hills: Sage Publications, 1979, pp. 99-117.
Collier, John Jr., *Vision Anthropology: Photography as a Research Method.* New York: Holt, Rinehart and Winston, 1967.
Vella, Jane. *Visual Aids for Nonformal Education.* Amherst: Center for International Education, 1979.Hills South, University of Massachusetts, 01003.

Photography: Sample

Photographing Events for Later Reflection

Perhaps the most poignant use of photos came when I was present to photograph a group experience and returned later with the photos for discussion. I was accompanying one literacy group on an all-day outing in the surrounding countryside. Historically, these illiterate residents had been deceived by the old hacienda owner who sold them their lots as agricultural land to avoid providing public space for parks and schools. Having walked two miles from the dry and crowded streets of their town that Sunday, they happened upon a golf course, owned by Swiss expatriates, the only green spot in the area.

We settled in a grove on the edge of the course for a quick picnic. Within ten minutes, the foreign proprietors were upon us, shaking angry clubs and shouting us off the land. Photographs of this confrontation served the following week as a stimulus to a discussion on the broader issue of property, evoking a critique of the historical conflict with the old landlord.

And why do foreigners have the only green piece of our land, they asked. The land issue turned out to be basic to this literacy group's very existence, when three months later, the class was expelled from its school meeting place by a principal, collaborating with the old hacienda owner.

From: Deborah Barndt, "Visual Interventions
in a Participatory Research Process: How a
Camera Can Enrich Interaction and Inquiry."
Participatory Research Project, International
Council for Adult Education, 1977

Useful Tools: **Problem Stories**

Definition:
In terms of project evaluation, problem stories are narrative accounts of past, present, or future situations that are used as a means to identify perceptions of project activities or impact, and as catalysts for discussion and analysis.

By using fictional characters, stories objectively or externalize problem situations. This often enables participants to be more honest in sharing their views and to gain a fuller understanding of the different points of view about a particular problem.

How It's Used:
Problem stories can be prepared by an outside evaluator to present to a group or by participants themselves (as individuals or groups). Stories can be written or taped.

As a measure of perception of project activities, problem stories can be used in a number of ways. Participants can be given a prepared story that depicts an event similar to a particular project event. Or, participants can be given a certain theme, such as "project leadership" or "cooperation," and make up their own stories. Also, participants might create stories about an "ideal" project and then contrast them with actual project activities.

To measure project impact, problem stories can provide effective pre-and post-tests. This can be done in two ways. First, participants can be asked to prepare a story on family or community life, both before and after a project. Second, participants can be presented with a problem situation at the beginning and end of a project. In both cases, comparisons can be made to determine what changes have occurred in the environment and in the participants.

Regardless of who prepares the story and the purpose for which it is used, group discussion is an important part of the evaluation process. Stories stimulate analysis and ideas that usually are applicable to real life situations. Stories prepared by participants may generate some useful data, but subsequent discussion is likely to generate even richer data. In addition, discussion can also be guided toward problem-solving and action-planning.

Using problem stories basically involves these steps: *presentation* of one or more stories to a group of no more than ten members (such as a project steering committee); *discussion/analysis* of the story (causes of the problem, what can be done about it, etc.); *generalizing* to the real life situation; and *planning* concrete actions to be taken.

Pros, Cons, Other Issues:
PROS: • Creative, insightful.
        • Adaptable for both literate and pre-literate groups.
        • Concrete; the story characters connect participants to their real life situations.
        • Usable as a pre/post test measure.

CONS: • Stories can be open to many interpretations.
        • Stories typically contain conflicts (personal conflicts, conflict of interests); when generalized to real-life, these may be difficult in some cases to resolve.

The evaluator using problem stories needs to have a sense of imagination and should be a skilled discussion leader.

Participatory Applications:
With problem stories, the most comprehensive evaluation data can be generated by involving participants in creating as well as analyzing. Having participants write or tape record their own stories is more time-consuming and less manageable than having a story on hand to which they can react. However, participant-created stories have several important advantages: they are accurate in depicting real and priority issues, they encompass diverse views, and they are more involving. All participants need not prepare stories, and the story author does not need to be revealed.

Another interesting participatory application is group story creation. In this case, creating and analyzing occur to some extent concurrently as participants discuss what to include and what not to include in their story.

Problem stories are really word photos of participants' reality, and they usually find much on which to comment. With this method, even shy or reticent participants will often be drawn into the discussion.

For More Information:
World Education. *AIM: A Creative Approach to Teaching Adults.* Boston: World Education, Inc., 210 Lincoln St. Mass. 02111.

Problem Stories: Sample

Dealing With Mr. Sam
I always shop at that corner market where Mr. Sam is most generous with his credit. Dealing with Mr. Sam, I don't have to wait until the first or the fifteenth to shop. I just go in anytime and get whatever I want. And when my check comes, I just turn it all over to Mr. Sam, to wipe out the credit and start all over again.

Dealing with Mr. Sam, you don't have to do a whole lot of planning and figuring things out before you go to the store. No. I can just run right across the street, pick up whatever I want, tell old man Sam to put it on the bill, and he is much obliging.

Sometimes, though, you have to be careful in picking things out because Mr. Sam don't like taking things back once you leave the store. No. Once you walk out that door, it's bought. Sometimes I stand at the vegetables fifteen, twenty minutes, just going through the tomatoes trying to find one with enough good parts left on it to make a nice tomato gravy. But it still beats all that planning and figuring.

And Mr. Sam is such a nice old man. Some people around here don't like him too much. They go up the street to that big supermarket where they are always having sales. To me, the little bit you save ain't hardly worth it. It takes a good fifteen minutes to walk clear over there. Then, too, you have to spend all that time figuring out what you are going to get and how much this costs and that costs. I don't have time for all that foolishness.

Now this woman who lives down the street from me, she is one of those who don't like Mr. Sam. I was in the store one day when she came in. Well, Mr. Sam cut this nice piece of roast for her and it didn't cost too much, either. But she stands there telling the man, "Now, you look here, Mr. Sam, I'm not buying your finger this morning. So you just take everything off that scale but the roast."   (Continues)

Mr. Sam was so mad he turned beet red. I felt so ashamed about that woman talking to Mr. Sam like that, nice as he is. So when she left, I just told him, "You can't deal with some of these people around here, 'cause they think they better than what they is. Got no respect." And he agreed.

"So what's your problem?" he asked. I showed him the pork chops he had sold to my little boy Jess. There were eleven slices. And every time Mr. Sam saw one with one of those little white worms on it he just took it out and put another slice in its place. He don't even bother to weigh it again and I could see some of the new slices were bigger than the ones he was taking out from mine and putting aside on the chopping block behind him. But he is nice that way. He'll give you a break.

Some woman who lives in this building next to mine organized this club and the woman comes every week to show them how to look through the newspaper and find the sales and make out a budget. She even tells them how many vitamins is in this and how many calories is in that and all that foolishness.

I don't have time for all that mess. I just run across the street to Mr. Sam, tell him what I want, and let him put it on the bill.

Story by Fred Hudson

I Love You Dad
"I don't give a damn, either your Dad goes to the rest home or I leave. I'm tired of cleaning crap off his sheets," Marcia said angrily.

"All right, all right," Bill shot back, pushing her away from the door. "We'll put him in the home, since you don't want the responsibility. I'll make the arrangements. Now get the hell out of my sight."

A week had passed since their argument. Bill had done nothing, and he and Marcia had hardly spoken to each other. Finally Marcia had told Bill that if he didn't call the rest home, she was going to do it herself. Bill had promised to look into it that day.

The house was very quiet. Out of habit Marcia glanced towards Dad's bedroom. It sure would be nice to be able to finish her cleaning without being interrupted. "I bet he calls me fifteen times a day. When he's gone, I'll have time to do my shopping and see my friends again," she thought.

All week Dad had seemed quiet except for what Marcia thought was sobbing. She would hear a sobbing noise coming from his bedroom when she was at that end of the house. "My God," she thought, "you wouldn't think a 74-year-old man would cry like that."

Thoughts Marcia had never before allowed herself to entertain, but that she had heard often enough from Bill, suddenly sprang into her mind. Dad was so old and the company of his family was all the pleasure he had. Making new friends wouldn't be easy. She would be his age herself someday. How would she feel?

Marcia had thought that taking care of Dad for nine months had been enough, but now she wondered if sending him to the home was really the best thing to do.

Story by Bill Sulentic

(Continues)

Doubts

As he stood there impatiently waiting for the next photograph to be taken, a thousand and one questions kept running through Miguel's mind. "What am I getting into? Will I have enough money to get her all the things she wants? Will I make her a good lover? A good husband? A good provider?"

As all these questions ran through Miguel's head, Gabriel, his best friend and best man, came up and interrupted his thoughts.

"What's the matter, buddy?" asked Gabriel. "Why the long face? Is anything wrong?"

"No," said Miguel. "I was just wondering about a lot of things. It is just beginning to hit me that I'm taking one of the most important steps in my life."

"Well, buddy, don't let that bother you too much. You've done pretty well up to now. And if I know you, you'll probably be able to take care of any problem that comes up," Gabe reassured his friend.

Miguel managed a smile. "You're probably right, Gabe."

"How about something to drink, buddy?" asked Gabe. "I know just the thing that'll make all your worries seem like nothing."

As Gabriel led him off to the side where the drinks were, Miguel struggled to put the doubts out of his mind.

Story by Joe Morales.
Stories from
AIM Project,
World Education, Inc.

Useful Tools: **Questionnaire**

Definition:
A questionnaire is a set of printed questions organized in a systematic way for the purpose of eliciting information from respondents. It is usually assumed to be a self-report mechanism, although questionnaires are frequently used in personal or telephone interviews. In the case of the latter, the questionnaires are referred to as "interview schedules." The questions may be open-ended (i.e., people respond in their own words), fixed-choice (i.e., people select a response from several alternatives), or projective (i.e., respondents pose solutions to problem situations).

How It's Used:
The first step in developing a questionnaire is deciding what information is needed for the evaluation. Once the parameters have been determined, a format must be selected for gathering this information. Some information is better gathered using open-ended questions while fixed-choice questions are more appropriate for others. The questions should be arranged in logical sequence, beginning with the easiest and least threatening.

Once a draft questionnaire has been developed, it should be pre-tested on a population similar to the one in which the study will be carried out. This will identify ambiguous questions, sensitive areas that should not be included in the questionnaire, and changes in the sequence of the questions.

The process of testing the questionnaire and rewriting the questions usually needs to be done several times before the final product is printed and used in the evaluation. If the information will be analyzed by computer, it is frequently helpful to develop a coding scheme for this purpose, as well.

If the questionnaire is administered to the respondents by interviewers, it is important to have some training sessions in which the interviewers can practice asking the questions in a systematic way.

Pros, Cons, Other Issues:
PROS: • Relatively inexpensive to administer since they can be completed without an interviewer being present.
 • The questions are standardized so each person receiving a copy is asked the same questions in the same way.
 • Questionnaires allow for more privacy, particularly if distributed by mail.
 • Well-designed questionnaires are easy to tabulate.

CONS: • Questionnaires have been over-used; people are tired of filling them out.
 • Nonliterates cannot use questionnaires without the assistance of another person.
 • Low rate of response.
 • Little opportunity to verify what people have said; many may not be telling the truth.

Participatory Applications:
Questionnaires are usually not considered to be very participatory. This can be changed by providing people in the group whose opinions are being elicited with the opportunity to help create the questionnaire. If the questionnaire is being administered in an interview setting, members of the group can also serve as interviewers and thereby increase their involvement. A more frequently used participatory technique is to present participants with the in-

formation that was gathered. Their opinions about what people said in the survey is an important part of what can be learned through this technique.

For More Information:
Anderson, Scarvia B.; Ball, Samuel; Murphy, Richard T. & Associates. "Questionnaires" — *Encyclopedia of Educational Evaluation.* San Francisco: Jossey-Bass Publishers, 1975. Excellent overview of evaluation concepts, including this one.

Questionnaire: Sample

An example of a questionnaire used by an interviewer in a group setting.

Region: Group's Name:
District: Facilitator:
Village: Date:

1. Age of members: _____

2. Sex of members: m _____ f _____

3. Is this group a church group? Yes _____ No _____

4. Has this group elected group leaders? Yes _____ No _____

    4a. If yes, who are they? _____
                        m _____ f _____

5. When did this group start? _____

6. How many members did the group have at the beginning? _____

7. How many members have left? _____
8. How many of the present members began with the group? _____
9. How often do you meet? _____
10. About how many members come to meetings? _____

11. Which literacy lessons have you covered? _____

12. Do you have a full-time facilitator? Yes _____ No _____
    12a. How often do you see him? _____
    12b. How much time does he spend with you?
    12c. What do you do with him? What do you talk about with him?

    _____

13. Do you have a volunteer facilitator? Yes _____ No _____
    13a. How often do you see him? _____
    13b. How much time does he spend with you? _____
    13c. What do you do with him? _____

14. Does the Village Development Committee know about your group? Yes _____ No _____
    14a. How do they know? _____
    14b. What do they think about your group? _____

                                                    (Continues)

15. Have you begun any self-help projects?   Yes _____   No _____
    15a. What are they?_____
    15b. Did you finish it/them?   Yes _____
    15c. If yes, how is it being ____ No _____ Other _____
    15d. If not completed, why not? _____
    15e. Did you have any problems with this project? _____
    15f. Who worked on it?   m _____   f _____
    15g. Who thought of the idea?   m _____   f _____

16. Do you have any other community projects? _____

28. How can you prevent malaria? _____

29. How can you prevent crop disease? _____

30. How much power would you say you have to improve your life?
        much   _____
        quite a bit _____
        some   _____
        very little _____
        none   _____

31. How do you think rural people can gain power to improve their lives?
    _____

32. How can you prevent your children from getting malnutrition?
    _____

33. When should you begin to give solid food to a baby?
        3 mos.   _____
        6 mos.   _____
        1 yr.   _____
        18 mos. _____

34. What do you do if your child gets diarrhea? _____

35. Do you think you can improve your income? Yes _____ No _____
    If yes, how? _____

37. What do you think can be done to improve the condition of feeder roads?
    _____

Prepared by
World Education Inc.
Monitoring Workshop Report
p. 54-6.

Useful Tools: **Scales**

Definition:
Scales encompass a variety of methods for rating, ranking, and categorizing reactions to what is being evaluated. Each instrument or tool includes a set of traits or descriptors that are to be arranged along a continuum of best to worst, most to least, etc. Most scales use written descriptors, but pictorial scales or simple verbal reactions can also be effective.

Some commonly used scales include checklists, rank orders, Q-sorts (cards containing descriptors to be sorted into a quasi-normal distribution), forced choice, ratings (often using a line divided into categories such as "always," "sometimes," "never"), and short reaction forms (e.g., "what I liked best"/"what I liked least.")

How It's Used:
PVOs interested in scales can utilize either already existing instruments (see sample) or "home-made" instruments. In general, it may be difficult to find scales appropriate for PVO projects, so constructing project-specific scales may be the best bet. Here are four typical scale formats: 1) classified: each statement or descriptor is rated according to a set of classifiers, such as "always," "sometimes," "never"; 2) descriptive: statements or descriptors are presented as a checklist or in groupings, of four or five, and those applicable are checked (usually, a forced choice must be made); 3) graphic: same as "classified" except that the set of classifiers are presented along a straight line continuum; and 4) defined group: statements or descriptors are arranged so that a specific proportion falls into assigned categories (in Q-sorts, specific numbers of cards must be arranged under each category heading; a parallel procedure could be used on a written form).

Scales are quite easy to use. With all scales, raters are basically asked to reflect on a project and to judge the project or aspects of it using the criteria presented. Raters can be individuals in separate locations (such as in their homes), individuals meeting in a common location (a community center), or groups. For groups, completing a scale involves reaching agreement among members on the ratings to be given. This process takes time but has other advantages (see "participatory applications").

The results of most scales can be compiled numerically, although with some scales, such as the Q-sort, compilation is a more complex process.

Pros, Cons, Other Issues:
PROS: • Clear, specific, focus.
         • Data easily recorded and compiled.
         • Eases comparison between/amongst projects.
         • Can deal with both quantitative or qualitative areas.
         • Requires mimimum of time and effort.

CONS: • May be difficult to find/construct an appropriate tool.
         • Generally, requires literacy skills.
         • Inconsistency from rater to rater, because individuals interpret statements differently.
         • Forced choice may be too limiting, present too narrow results.

In developing statements and descriptions to be included in a scale, it is important to be as specific as possible. Considerable detail, including examples, promotes more consistent understanding of the traits amongst the raters. For instance, along with the statement, "I have improved my leadership abilities," include some examples of effective leadership behavior.

Participatory Applications:

Scales are most typically *developed* by "expert" evaluators, *administered* by evaluators, *taken* by individual community members, and *compiled* by the evaluators. By involving community members in each of these four steps, however, scales become an effective participatory tool.

Community members can make a valuable contribution to the construction of a scale by contributing their ideas of the traits to include. Group brainstorming sessions can be held, based on a goal or task analysis format to provide some structure.

If the scale is to be taken by individuals, community members can also be involved in administration. Much fuller participation occurs, though, if a group works on completing a scale together. Needless to say, this process generates much discussion, analysis, even debate. Thus, the rating or evaluation activity becomes a means to share different opinions on project strengths and weaknesses and to agree on future directions. The process actually includes the two steps of compiling the scale and taking the scale. In contrast to the individual approach to using scales, the group approach enables community members to reflect, analyze, and chart a course of action together; it promotes their greater community control over project decisions.

When group rating may not seem appropriate or feasible for some reason, community members can still be involved in compiling results. For instance, a community evaluation team might jointly record the scale responses and then present the outcomes at a community meeting.

For More Information:

Nunnally, Jim C. *Educational Measurement and Evaluation.* New York: McGraw Hill, 1972.
Nunnally, Jim C. *Tests and Measurements: Assessment and Prediction.* New York: McGraw Hill, 1959.
Thorndike, Robert L. and Hagen, Elizabeth. *Measurement and Evaluation in Psychology and Evaluation in Psychology and Evaluation.* New York: John Wiley and Sons, 1966.

Scales: Sample

COMMUNITY SOLIDARITY INDEX

VARIABLE MEASURED: Amount of consensus among members
of primary rural communities
(250-2000 Population)

DESCRIPTION: Eight major areas of community
behaviour are examined.

1. Community spirit
2. Interpersonal relations
3. Family responsibility toward the community
4. Schools
5. Religious institutions
6. Economic behaviour
7. Local government
8. Tension areas

These eight areas are covered in a series of 40 statements that are rated by the respondent on a five-item scale according to his judgement of how the statements apply to this community. The items range from "very true" to "definitely untrue" with scores ranging from 5 for the "very true" response to 1 for the "definitely untrue" response. The standard deviation of the scores of all the schedules for the community is taken as a measure of the degree of consensus and, therefore, of solidarity in the community. The smaller the S the greater the solidarity is assumed to be. The mean of the total score is considered to be an index of the members' opinion of the quality for the community. For comparison with other commnities an octagonal profile may be used.

COMMUNITY SOLIDARITY INDEX SCHEDULE

Name _____ Age _____

Community _____ Occupation _____

Married _____ Single _____

If married, number of children in school, if any _____

boys _____ girls _____, number of children out of

school_____ Location of residence in town _____

_____ Outside of town _____

how far _____ miles/kilometers?

Think of each of the statements below as relating to the people of this entire community both in town and in neighbouring villages. If you think the statement fits this community very well, after the statement circle vt (for very true); if it applies only partially, circle t (for true); If you can not see how it relates one way or another to this particular community, circle nd (for not decided); if you think it is not true, circle u (for untrue); and if it definitely is not true, circle du (for definitely untrue). PLEASE RECORD THE IMPRESSION THAT FIRST OCCURS TO YOU.

Do not go back and change your answers.

(Continues)

1. Real friends are hard to find in this community.
    vt   t   nd   u   du   (2)

2. Our schools do a poor job of preparing young people for life.
    vt   t   nd   u   du   (4)

3. Local concerns deal fairly and squarely with everyone.
    vt   t   nd   u   du   (6)

4. The community is very peaceful and orderly.
    vt   t   nd   u   du   (8)

    The number in parentheses indicates the area to which the statements belongs.

5. A lot of people here think they are too nice for you.
    vt   t   nd   u   du   (1)

6. Families in this community keep their children under control.
    vt   t   nd   u   du   (3)

7. The different religious institutions here cooperate well with one another.
    vt   t   nd   u   du   (5)

8. Some people here "get by with murder" while others take the rap for any little misdeed.
    vt   t   nd   u   du   (7)

9. Almost everyone is polite and courteous to you.
    vt   t   nd   u   du   (2)

10. Our schools do a good job of preparing students for college.
    vt   t   nd   u   du   (4)

11. Everyone here tries to take advantage of you.
    vt   t   nd   u   du   (6)

12. People around here show good judgment.
    vt   t   nd   u   du   (8)

13. People won't work together to get things done for the community.
    vt   t   nd   u   du   (1)

14. Parents teach their children to respect other people's rights and property.
    vt   t   nd   u   du   (3)

15. Most of our religious minded people forget the meaning of the word brotherhood when they get out of their religious institutions.
    vt   t   nd   u   du   (5)

16. This community lacks real leaders.
    vt   t   nd   u   du   (7)

17. People give you a bad name if you insist in being different.
    vt   t   nd   u   du   (2)

18. Our high school students take an active interest in making their community a better place in which to live.
    vt   t   nd   u   du   (4)

19. A few people here make all the money.
    vt   t   nd   u   du   (6)

20. Too many young people get into sex difficulties.
    vt   t   nd   u   du   (8)

(Continues)

21. The community tries hard to help its young people along.
    vt   t   nd   u   du   (1)

22. Folks are unconcerned about what their kids do so long as they keep out of trouble.
    vt   t   nd   u   du   (3)

23. The religious institutions here are a constructive factor for better community life.
    vt   t   nd   u   du   (5)

24. The civic office bearers run the town/village to suit themselves.
    vt   t   nd   u   du   (7)

25. I feel very much that I belong here.
    vt   t   nd   u   du   (2)

26. Many young people in the community do not finish high school.
    vt   t   nd   u   du   (4)

27. The people here are all money pinchers.
    vt   t   nd   u   du   (6)

28. You must spend lots of money to be accepted here.
    vt   t   nd   u   du   (8)

29. The people as a whole mind their own business.
    vt   t   nd   u   du   (1)

30. Most people get their families to attend religious institutions on religious occasions.
    vt   t   nd   u   du   (3)

31. Every religious institution wants to be the biggest and the most impressive.
    vt   t   nd   u   du   (5)

32. A few have the town/village politics well sewed up.
    vt   t   nd   u   du   (7)

33. Most of the students here learn to read and write well.
    vt   t   nd   u   du   (4)

34. People are generally critical of others.
    vt   t   nd   u   du   (2)

35. Local concerns expect their help to live on low wages.
    vt   t   nd   u   du   (6)

36. You are out of luck here if you happen to be of the wrong caste.
    vt   t   nd   u   du   (8)

37. No one seems to care much how the community looks.
    vt   t   nd   u   du   (1)

38. If their children keep out of the way, parents are satisfied to let them do whatever they want to do.
    vt   t   nd   u   du   (3)

39. Most of our religious minded people do not practice what they preach.
    vt   t   nd   u   du   (5)

From:
Participatory Research, A Frame of
Reference," Dr. Joseph Singh, A Working
Paper Prepared by the Development Division
of CASA, New Delhi, undated.

Useful Tools: **Unobtrusive Measures**

Definition:
The use of unobtrusive measures involves gathering information about a community or situation without the knowledge or consent of the people in that setting. The infomation, usually obtained inconspicuously, may include physical traces, archives and personal observations.

How It's Used:
Unobtrusive measures are used to gather information without disturbing people. Researchers have demonstrated that people react differently when they realize someone is gathering data regarding their behavior. The task, therefore, is to gather this information inconspicuously

Observing physical traces involves examining behavioral evidence. For example, instead of asking people whether they use latrines, one could count the number of village latrines with paths that are overgrown with grass. Similarly, the wear and tear on a library book will reflect the extent of its use.

The records kept in a society are also a good source of information. For example, morbidity and mortality rates should reflect whether a community health program has resulted in changed behavior. Diaries, letters, personal logs and agency records can also tell the evaluator about community life and the effect of local programs.

Systematically recorded observations can also provide important information for evaluation purposes. Tape recorders, still cameras, television and movie projectors can be used instead of human observers.

Pros, Cons, Other Issues:
PROS: • Information already exists, and can be collected economically.
         • Behavior of people in the community is not affected by the process of gathering information.

CONS: • Easy to misinterpret physical evidence.
         • Existing records are notoriously poor in many countries.

A secretive approach raises serious ethical problems. Research reports based on information gathered without the knowledge or consent of those involved may embarrass or even endanger organizations or communities being studied.

Participatory Applications:
Although the use of unobtrusive measures was designed primarily to help outside observers learn about the life of a community without causing people to change their behavior, participation in the process is still possible. People in a community may be invited to look at their own circumstances, sharing in the search for appropriate evaluative information. Alternatively, if this information is gathered by outside observers, the conclusions may be presented to community groups in a context within which they are able to discuss the findings and address the implications.

For More Information:
Anderson, Scarvia B.; Ball, Samuel; Murphy, Richard T. and Associates. "Unobtrusive Measures." *Encyclopedia of Educational Evaluation.* San Francisco: Jossey-Bass Publishers, 1975. An excellent overview of evaluation concepts, including this one.

Webb, Eugene.; Campbell, David T.; Schwartz, Richard D.; and Sechrest, Lee. *Unobtrusive Measures: Nonreactive Research in the Social Sciences.* Chicago; Rand McNally & Co., 1972. The classic book on the use of unobtrusive measures.

CHAPTER SIX

SOME THOUGHTS ON EVALUATION UTILIZATION

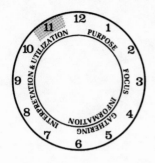

The file drawer may be one of the major hazards to evaluation. What could be more futile than to collect a ream of good evaluation information, have it read and discussed, and then filed and forgotten. That has happened all too often. Hence, in a sourcebook on evaluation, it is vitally important to address the issue of evaluation utilization — using evaluation to make decisions and to direct actions that will improve a project.

George Gershwin summarized the purpose of evaluation succinctly: Accentuate the positive, eliminate the negative. The purpose of evaluation is to identify the strengths of program activities and outcomes so they can be re-enforced or replicated, while at the same time identifying weaknesses so they may be minimized. It is a process that takes brutal honesty, calling for more than description, no matter how precise; it requires the making of judgments. The utilization process, then, goes on to make decisions based on those judgments, and to take actions based on those decisions.

The process is so simple and obvious that it may seem unnecessary to describe — it may be assumed to happen automatically. But such is not the case. Each step in the process is a point at which evaluation is vulnerable to inaction and could be rendered useless — or at least unused.

The Role of Judgments
A judgment is a statement of worth about something. Descriptions often imply judgments. For example, a description of an achieved objective would seem to imply a positive judgment. And descriptions of objectives that are not accomplished carry an assumed negative judgment.

To make assumptions about worth is dangerous, however. Judgments should be made rationally and systematically, as if one were collecting information.

1) A model for evaluative judgments. It is useful to visualize evaluation using a two-by-two matrix that compares accomplishments to values. (See Figure #1.) Cell 1 in the matrix suggests that some accomplishments, both planned and unplanned, are GOOD. It would be nice if all activity and accomplishment would turn out to be GOOD, but that is not the case. Cell 2 suggests that some outcomes accomplished during a program may not be good. For instance, a project in India encouraged a village to raise fish. So much attention was given to the village that neighboring villages became incensed and one night poisoned the fishpond. That was an unplanned outcome that was not good and is worth avoiding in the future.

Figure #1

Activities/Outcomes

	Accomplished		Non-accomplished
	Planned	Unplanned	
good		1	4
	Planned	Unplanned	
bad		2	3

Evaluation Judgment Matrix

Cells 3 and 4 suggest that non-accomplished outcomes can be judged either good or bad. It is often assumed that failure to accomplish a planned outcome is bad (Cell 3). But planners are not omniscient. Some planned outcomes might be better never accomplished. Therefore, failure to accomplish those outcomes would be good (Cell 4). A leprosy control program in West Africa set its objectives to provide inpatient care for needy leprosy patients. But they found that needy patients refused the care. In frustration, they surveyed leprosy patients to find out why they would not come to the hospital. One discovery was that if patients came to the hospital for the periods of time necessary to receive the treatment, they would lose their crops, land and homes. In light of this new insight, the staff felt it was good that they did not accomplish their objectives as originally designed. They changed their approach, wrote new objectives, and implemented a program that offered treatment to patients in their homes. Patients gladly received treatment under the new plan.

This example points out that the measurement of accomplishment and a description of activities are only steps in the evaluation process. It is important to go beyond description and to make judgments whether those activities and outcomes are worthwhile. Only when a judgment is made will it be clear what action should take place as a result of the evaluation.

2) *The need for stated values.* In order to make useful judgments it is necessary to have a well-articulated value position. This may be a philosophy of development or a kind of doctrinal statement of development. Values are often implicit in well defined statements of goals and objectives. But sometimes it is important to go beyond such statements of goals and objectives and articulate our beliefs.

In Section I we suggested five fundamental value items of a philosophical nature shared by most PVOs.

1) *People are responsible for their own development.*

2) *Change is possible.*

3) *Change occurs in community.*

4) *Development is growth.*

5) *Development workers are enablers.*

A number of development agencies can subscribe to these value statements. Other organizational values will be specific to a single agency, but need to be stated nonetheless. Following are some examples of organization-specific value statements associated with PVOs:

- Grain production will help solve the world's food shortage.
- Animal production will help solve the world's food shortage.
- Child needs must be met at the community level.
- Child needs must be met at the family level.
- Child development must enable children to become fulfilled adults.
- It is important to enable local organizations in order that health projects be long-lasting and locally maintained.
- Education (learning) is essential to every development project.
- The local church must be involved in community development.
- Catholics and Protestants must work together in promoting development.

Both the general statements and those that apply to a specific organization become value standards against which accomplishments or non-accomplishments are judged. They should be in writing so they may be applied to judgments uniformly.

3) The need for shared values. Threat is a major problem in evalua-tion. A staff may feel threatened because they do not know what stand-ards will be used to judge their work. For this reason, it is important that the staff and evaluators share a common value position.

Many evaluations fail over this issue, particularly when ouside evaluators are brought into a project. Outsiders seldom share fully the values of the project members. Hence, judgments frequently are made or implied on the basis of divergent value systems.

Another problem arises when donor agencies do not share values of an implementing agency. One agency agreed with a donor on a plan to im-plement a number of local-level health projects. Both agreed on the value of local in-country organizations learning to implement small projects. But shortly after the program started the grantee recognized that they had underestimated the amount of time and effort it would take to enable local agencies to implement the projects. They adjusted their plan and time frame. The donor agency, however, was much less committed to the value of local organization deveopment than to highly visible local project activities. A great deal of stress developed between the donor agency and the grantee. They simply did not share the same values.

Throughout the evaluation process, values as well as accomplishments should be brought under scrutiny. All parties related to the project — staff, beneficiaries, evaluators, and donors — have a role in articu-lating these values. That may require some negotiating. But negotia-tions can be a healthy process. Evaluation must be supported by a solid foundation of shared values. In this way, measured evidence of ac-complishment or non-accomplishment will be judged similarly by donors, PVOs, community people and others related to the project.

Turning Judgments into Action
Judgments are statements of worth; decisions are statements of action. Evaluation without action is not worth the exercise. Therefore, judgments must be translated into decisions, and decisions must be translated into action. The following organizational qualities will enhance that process.

1) Commitment to quality. A staff that is committed to quality and effectiveness is more likely to implement actions based on evaluation judgments than is a staff committed to something else. To say it rather bluntly, a commitment to ego or empire building will interfere with ra-tional evaluation decisions and action. Likewise, a genuine commit-ment to quality is different in a highly politicized organization in which members are recognized and promoted by playing the "political game." It might be wise to assess these qualities in a project organization before beginning the evaluation process. If they exist, don't even start to evaluate.

2) *Decision structure.* An important question to ask of any organization is: Who makes what decisions? While there are various decision-making structures in organizations, one must be in place for evaluation decisions to be made and implemented. If staff members do not know who is responsible for making decisions, particularly decisions that initiate change, then those decisions will probably not be made. Uncertainty about decision-making authority develops from situations in which decisions made by staff are frequently overturned or modified by someone else in the organization. Where an uncertain climate exists, staff members tend to make only the safe, routine decisions and to "bump" more consequential decisions up the organization. When decisions are continually "bumped up," the result is that a decision overload eventually develops at some point in the organization. The result is that some decisions don't get made and others are not followed up. Evaluation decisions are neither routine nor safe. They need a sound decision structure to make them, to implement them and to support them.

3) *A case for participation.* The evaluation utilization process involves three groups: those who make judgments, those who make decisions, and those who implement actions. In some organizations these groups will overlap. In others they may remain distinct. When the staff members who are responsible for action share in making decisions and judgments, evaluation decisions will be more effectively implemented. Conversely, when the people responsible for action do not share in making decisions and judgments, action implementation will be less effective. There is a strong case for broad participation in the whole evaluation process.

Just as a runner does not finish a marathon until he's taken the last step across the finish line, so evaluation is not complete until judgments and decisions have been made and action implemented. In planning evaluation, it is important to also plan for utilization. Design your evaluation so as to enhance utilization, and involve in it the people who are crucial to utilization.

WHAT TO DO
WHEN YOU NEED HELP

INTRODUCTION

No publication on evaluation can possibly enter into all the related issues of the field or the appropriateness for every audience. Our choice of material reflects our own experience as PVO practitioners and what we believe is most relevent to our colleagues. In this section, we want to leave our readers with practical suggestions for seeking further help and information.

The three areas we explore are:

1. *Selecting an Outside Consultant.*

2. *Collaborative PVO Efforts: the "Approaches to Evaluation" Project.*

3. *A Working Bibliography.*

Our information is not intended to be comprehensive, but it is sufficient to meet the needs of most PVO practitioners. As your experience grows, most certainly your options will expand, so remember, this information is subject to constant change.

CHAPTER ONE
SELECTING AN OUTSIDE CONSULTANT

Selecting an Outside Consultant

The Sourcebook has been biased towards the development of PVO's internal capability to design and conduct program evaluations. But our orientation is not exclusionary. There are moments when an outside consultant is necessary.

Outsiders are considered to offer the greatest possibility for objectivity, and may be required by a donor for just this reason. The project itself may merit it because of the significance of the decisions that need to be made or, due to certain complexities, the evaluation is felt to be beyond the staff's capability. Outside evaluators often have highly specialized training and can provide a broader perspective, drawing parallels with other programs in the same field. They can stimulate a fundamental rethinking of program assumptions by taking a fresh look at what has become too familiar to those involved.

An outsider can occasionally serve quite usefully as a facilitator between the respective parties to the evaluation. Our relationships with local project holders, participants, donors, and host governments are complex and delicate. An independent figure with considerable authority can carry off an evaluation which would falter otherwise due to inter-institutional relationships. Finally, outsiders are useful for instilling public confidence and enhancing our image with U.S. constituencies that contribute to our programs.

Once the decision has been made to hire an outside evaluator, the next step is selecting the appropriate one to meet the needs of your particular project and audience. In this section, we offer some ideas of how to go about this difficult task. You should also feel free to seek references from colleagues who have faced similar situations and advertise in pertinent publications. Whatever method you choose to initiate the search, there are a number of factors that need to be considered before the hunt begins.

On pages 26-28 *A Self Examination*, practical guides are offered to help the PVO practitioner decide whether outside evaluation assistance is needed. The framework described by the Evaluation Clock presumes that whether or not an outside evaluator is contracted, PVO staff will be intimately involved in each phase. Therefore, the qualities of an evaluator are critical.

Dr. Richard R. Johnson, Research Director of the Exxon Educational Foundation, provided important advice on the question of outside evaluation at our Wingspread Conference. He has generously allowed us to reprint the following excerpt from his introduction to the *Directory of Evaluation Consultants*, published by the Foundation Center, which furnishes a checklist to consider before contracting any evaluator.

Qualities of Evaluators

There are a number of qualities and capacities which evaluators have in differing amounts. Depending upon the purpose of the evaluation, you might set radically different priorities among these qualities. The following list can be used to note those that are absolutely essential, others which are desirable and still others which may be of lesser importance. In this way job specification can be set up before the search begins for the evaluator.

- *Knowledge/Skill Base:* Evaluators have different backgrounds. In some cases it may be crucial to have individuals on the evaluation team with knowledge in the particular subject matter area, experience in dealing with a particular age group or ethnic population, or background in working with a particular kind of an organization or institution. By the same token, some kinds of studies require very specific skills such as experience in survey construction, statistical analysis of data or depth interviewing. Indeed, one of the common reasons for seeking an outside consultant in evaluation is to secure a particular skill that the client lacks. But beware of deciding too quickly on a particular technique of gathering information such as conducting a survey, and in so doing, ruling out other, possibly useful, individuals. It is important to consider carefully how crucial any skill or knowledge is to the proposed evaluation before using it as a screening device.

  It should be noted that the skills the evaluator possesses may also *constrain* the kind of evaluation developed. The "Law of the Hammer" says: *"Give a small boy a hammer and he will discover that everything needs to be pounded."* In the same way an evaluator highly skilled in survey research, for example, may think all evaluation requires some form of opinion sampling. Thus, you should consider the skills of the evaluator, but not constrain the search for a consultant too early by this criterion. At the same time, do not merely list the skills of evaluators and "buy the one with the most accessories."

(Continues)

- *Authority:* All evaluators are expected to report to or communicate with some audience. You must therefore consider what kind of authority the evaluator must carry, given the audience for the evaluation and the kinds of decisions to be influenced. Sometimes authority is related to credentials and skills. At other times it reflects group membership or track record and eminence in a field. The importance of the evaluator's authority must be weighed against other qualities needed for your project. If the evaluator is to provide feedback and "management consulting" to the project, interpersonal skills and sensitivity to the personal relations and the politics of the project may be more important. However, if authority will be a crucial issue in an evaluation, it needs to be taken into account in selecting the evaluator.

- *Communication:* A special skill that deserves to be considered separately from skills related to data collection and analysis is the ability to communicate. Many evaluations go unused because the mode, style, or timing (e.g., providing a report for decision-making after the decision has been made) of the evaluation report are inappropriate for the target audience. Much of the present evaluation literature is still influenced by academic research reporting styles. In many cases this style does not speak to the audience. For some evaluations, the style and mode of communicating may be as critical as the content. In all cases it is well to consider how important both oral and written communication will be to the impact of the evaluation and to assess the evaluator accordingly.

- *Style:* Evaluators with roughly the same knowledge and skill base who work with similar evaluation models may nevertheless have different personal styles. One dimension in which evaluators vary is their stance toward the client. A large proportion of traditional evaluators come out of training in research fields and prefer a relationship with granting agencies and clients that resembles the "basic research" model. Once the client has specified the problem (which the evaluator may wish to help shape), they assume that they should be turned loose to design and conduct the evaluation. These evaluators see their main obligation as producing an acceptable report to be turned in at the end of the evaluation period. Such individuals prefer grants, relatively little interference from the client and often very little interaction with the client as well.

Another set of evaluators expects far more interaction with the client. They are also comfortable with an RFP (Request For Proposal) as a funding process. With the proposal-grant mechanism, the client follows the model of funding basic research, leaving the scientist free to do his or her research. In contrast, the RFP model of funding is more like hiring an architect to design a house. Not only is the problem specified, but the scope of funding and some of the constraints on acceptable solutions are laid out. An evaluator responding to an RFP

(Continues)

submits a design within specified limits in competition with other evaluators. With this style of evaluation, the consultant also expects more interaction with the client during the evaluation process.

Another group of evaluators prefers to negotiate not only problem scope and evaluation design with a client, but also plans to involve the client in data collection and interpretation. In this third style of interaction, the ongoing relationship between client and evaluator may be formalized by an evaluation contract.

You should also note the deep division within the field of evaluation concerning who should put the "value" in evaluation. No sophisticated evaluator would argue for complete objectivity in evaluation. But acknowledging this limitation leads to very different styles of evaluation for different individuals. There is a significant group, largely continuing within the framework of the scientific model, that seeks to approximate objectivity. For these individuals, the task is to provide "just the facts" in order to help the decision maker make a judgment. The presumption is that by disclosure of method and cross-critique of evaluations, greater objectivity can be approached. The "value" comes when the client or decision maker uses the evaluation report in a particlar way.

A second group, recognizing that true objectivity is impossible, maintains that the "value" should be included within the evaluation process. The argument is that no evaluator can present a report free of his or her values and that, furthermore, it is the responsibility of the evaluator to come to some conclusion about the value of the program being evaluated. Under these conditions the evaluation report may contain explicit recommendations to the decisionmaker. While the decisionmaker is still free to make a contrary judgment, the situation presented with this style of evaluation is really quite different.

- *Logistics:* The logistics of involving any person or group in an evaluation also need to be considered. There are obvious issues such as the geographic distance of evaluators from the program sites or the client, as well as evaluator access to needed equipment such as computers. Another factor often overlooked in choosing evaluators is competition for time. Some evaluators become overcommitted and performance on a given evaluation suffers. It is a good idea to get a full assessment of the evaluator's other activities and commitments during the period contemplated for the evaluation.

- *Links:* Evaluators do not come in hermetically sealed packages. In considering various candidates for conducting an evaluation, it is important to see the context in which they are embedded as well as their individual characteristics. Being a member of a particular university

(Continues)

faculty or a particular research group may affect the evaluation just as being a member of a political or ideological group could influence the process. The past track record in working with advocacy groups or professional associations could be germane to how the evaluation is conducted or how the evaluation report will be received.

The various qualities and competencies mentioned above are not independent of one another, nor are they exhaustive in describing the various ways evaluators may differ. What they do offer, however, is a way of organizing the planning which ought to occur *before* you begin looking for an evaluation consultant. In this way a number of criteria for selection can be set up to allow screening of potential evaluators.

Where to Look for Consultants

The task of identifying an appropriate outside evaluator can be difficult. One of the concrete proposals to emerge from the Wingspread Conference is a plan to form an information bank on evaluation consultants. The bank will require participating PVOs to contribute information on positive experiences with consultants and, in return, gain access to this rich pool of information on where to look for outside assistance.

There is no one predominant pattern of PVOs seeking outside consultants. There are three sources worth discussing in detail: U.S. groups, Third World organizations, and individual consultants.

1) *United States Evaluation Groups.* A casual look at the *Directory of Evaluation Consultants*, will convince anyone that evaluation is a thriving business. Most of the listed organizations have served large-scale government programs, and work in proximity to large universities where they recruit their personnel. PVOs have generally not sought their assistance.

There are, however, some professional groups that have worked extensively with PVOs, often through contracts with the Agency for International Development (AID). The New Trans-Century Foundation, which has provided both training and specific evaluation consultancy is a leading example. A new initiative, which seeks to close the gap between PVO and university expertise is the Joint PVO/Rural Development Center of Western Carolina University. Evaluation is one of various interests they hope to develop with PVOs. For further information write to the Center in Cullowhee, North Carolina 28723.

Actual working relations have often been barriers to taking full advantage of specialized forms of assistance. Where the donor mandates the use of an outside evaluator, the fear of him/her imposing different values can outweight the potential benefits of professional research. The only safeguard, of course, is control of the evaluation process, which PVOs will maintain more securely as they develop their own internal systems.

2) *Third World Organizations.* There is no easy guide to these organizations. Many PVOs prefer the cultural advantage a local evaluator will have. Our project did not involve this category of practitioners to the extent we wanted. It is an important category for the sharing of information among PVOs to identify potential resources.

3) *Individual Consultants.* The most common form of outside evaluation assistance is the individual consultant. Such service is not only easier to manage and use in specific phases of the evaluation process, but can be located in diverse ways. In recent years, a cadre of independent consultants, often with extensive familiarity of PVO programs, has developed. Sharing information about such persons would alleviate the problem of finding the right person.

An underutilized alternative to independent consultants is the exchange of staff among PVOs. This form of consultancy could occur in various ways. In the field, a qualified staff member of one agency might participate in an evaluation team of another agency. In headquarters, an experienced evaluator in one agency could participate in the design of evaluations or analysis of information from the field. In either case, the resulting cost savings and the advantages of learning from each other's experience are important attractions. In addition, the evaluation will benefit from added objectivity and needed outside expertise.

Although we have not provided easy answers on how to find outside assistance, this question is a priority concern of this project. The more experience and confidence we gain in evaluation, the more we will get out of the evaluation process. The better we understand what we want from outside assistance, the easier it will be to find appropriate human resources.

CHAPTER TWO

COLLABORATIVE PVO EFFORTS

From its inception, the "Approaches to Evaluation" Project nurtured a collaborative spirit among PVOs. The framework for evaluation described in this sourcebook stresses learning in community — it is a call to make our service to the communities in the developing world a dynamic combination of doing and learning. We have also suggested ways to make this spirit a working reality, including sharing of evaluation experiences, comparing lessons learned and exchanging staff for evaluation. This project, under the auspices of the ACVAFS, will continue its role as a facilitator of joint action. Among areas we are planning for further action are:

1. Training opportunities in the United States and overseas to allow PVO staff to deepen their understanding of evaluation.

2. Extensive networking to disseminate information and facilitate learning opportunities for PVO staff. These opportunities will center on an analysis of evaluation results and issues, e.g., evaluation of primary health programs or achieving maximum community participation.

3. Establishment of a consultancy information bank and support for appropriate evaluation initiatives.

These activities depend on the interest and initiative of participating PVOs. They can only thrive in an atmosphere of open dialogue, and, therefore, we welcome your suggestions concerning our activities.

As part of this objective, we are including a list of contact persons in the agencies who have participated in the project's development. They are staff who have both responsibility for evaluation and an interest in the collaborative process.

George A. Reagan
Agricultural Cooperative Development Intl.
201 Continental Building
1012 14th Street N.W.
Washington, DC 20005

Patricia Hunt
American Friends Service Committee
1501 Cherry Street
Philadelphia, PA 19102

Sherwood B. Slater
American Jewish Joint
Distribution Committee
60 East 42nd Street.
Suite 1914
New York, NY 10165

Ray Rignall
CARE
660 First Avenue
New York, NY 10016

William Pruzensky
Catholic Relief Services
(U.S. Catholic Conference)
1011 First Avenue
New York, NY 10022

Alfred Watts
Christian Children's Fund
P.O. Box 26511
Richmond, VA 23261

Nancy Nicalo
Church World Service
475 Riverside Drive
New York, NY 10115-0050

Kenneth Brown
CODEL
79 Madison Avenue
New York, NY 10157

Donald Miller
Compassion International
Box 7000
Colorado Springs, CO 80933

Bruce Woodcock
The Episcopal Church
in the U.S.A.
815 Second Avenue
New York, NY 10017

Than Nguyen
Family Farm Development Network
c/o Heifer Project International
P.O. Box 808
825 West 3rd Street
Little Rock, AR 72203

Anthony DiBella
Foster Parents Plan International
155 Plan Way
Warwick, RI 02887

Bernard Hosie
Foundation for Peoples of
the South Pacific
P.O. Box 1746
La Jolla, CA 92038

Robert Ransom
Goodwill Industries
of America
International Department
9200 Wisconsin Avenue
Bethesda, MD 20814

Armin Schmidt
Heifer Project International
P.O. Box 808
Little Rock, AR 72203

Ron Texley
Helen Keller International
15 West 16th Street
New York, NY 10011

Phil Canada
Institute for International
Development
360 Maple Avenue West, Suite F
Vienna, VA 22180

Heather Clark
International Voluntary Services
1424 16th Street N.W.
Washington, DC 20010

Joseph Sprunger
Lutheran World Relief
360 Park Avenue South
New York, NY 10010

Merrill Ewert
MAP International
P.O. Box 50
Wheaton, IL 60187

Cheryl Allam
Maryknoll Sisters
Research & Planning
P.O. Box 534
Maryknoll, NY 10545

Richard Redder
Meals for Millions/Freedom
from Hunger Foundation
P.O. Box 2000
Davis, CA 95616

Suzanne Kindervatter
Overseas Education Fund
2101 L Street N.W., Suite 916
Washington, DC 20037

Arlene Lear
ORT (American ORT Federation)
817 Broadway
New York, NY 10003

Leslie Tuttle
OXFAM America
115 Broadway
Boston, MA 02116

Sandra Rivers
**Family Planning
International Assistance
Planned Parenthood Federation**
810 Seventh Avenue
New York, NY 10019

Carolyn Stremlau
PACT
777 United Nations Plaza
New York, NY 10017

John Wiggins
**The Salvation Army World
Service Office**
1025 Vermont Avenue N.W.
Washington, DC 20005

Jairo Arboleda
Save The Children
54 Wilton Road
Westport, CT 06880

David Syme
**Seventh Day Adventist
World Service**
6840 Eastern Avenue N.W.
Washington, DC 20012

Timothy Brendle
**Southern Baptist Convention/
Foreign Mission Board**
P.O. Box 6597
Richmond, VA 23230

James Herne
TECHNOSERVE
11 Belden Avenue
Norwalk, CT 06851

Jim Ekstrom
**Town Affiliation
Association of U.S.**
Sister Cities International
1625 Eye St. N.W.
Washington, DC 20006

Elizabeth Coit
**Unitarian Universalist
Service Committee**
78 Beacon Street
Boston, MA 02108

Beth Heisey
**United Methodist Committee
on Relief**
475 Riverside Drive
New York, NY 10015

Alice Gerlach
Volunteers in Technical Assistance
3706 Rhode Island Avenue
Mt. Rainier, MD 20822

Jeanne McCormack
World Education
210 Lincoln Street
Boston, MA 02111

Jim Rugh
World Neighbors
5116 N. Portland Avenue
Oklahoma City, OK 73112

David Chambers
World Relief Corporation
P.O. Box WRC
Wheaton, IL 60187

Bill Warnock
World Vision International
919 W. Huntington Drive
Monrovia, CA 91016

Steve LaVake
Young Men's Christian Association
101 North Wacker Drive
Chicago, IL 60606

CHAPTER THREE
WORKING BIBLIOGRAPHY

The following bibliography seeks to encourage the PVO practitioner to develop his/her own sources of information. It reflects our experience in carrying out this project and our best advice on where to look for further guidance. Wherever possible, we have included not only annotated references, but also where to write to obtain information.

The bibliography is organized into the following categories:

1. ACVAFS Publications
2. Private and Voluntary Organization Material
3. Priority Evaluation Texts
4. Background Evaluation Literature
5. Colleague Agency and Other Source Material

The reference number (REF. 1) that follow citations in the text indicates the category where the source is listed. Note that the bibliography does not repeat all the references given in the text.

All the publications included in the bibliography with the exception of those in category 4 are available for reference in the ACVAFS/TAICH office, 200 Park Avenue South, New York City. We intend to expand this collection, especially unpublished material and publications from the PVO community. Contributions will be warmly appreciated.

1. American Council of Voluntary Agencies for Foreign Service Publications

ACVAFS, "Evaluation in the PVO Community," 1979.

ACVAFS, "A Working Report on Monitoring in the PVO Community," May 1981.

ACVAFS, "A Report of a Workshop on Impact Evaluation," October 1981.

ACVAFS, "Evaluation — Its Implications for Voluntary Agency Program Policy" (Wingspread Conference), March 1982.

All these publications resulted from the "Approaches to Evaluation" Project. Single copies are available upon request from ACVAFS, 200 Park Avenue South, New York, NY 10003.

2. Private Voluntary Organization Publications

American Friends Service Committee, *Tin Aicha, Nomad Village.*
Philadelphia: AFSC — International Division, 1982.

A report on AFSC's involvement over several years in a region of
Mali devastated by the Sahelian drought. It contains a detailed
description of the project, a summary of field evaluation, and
lessons for AFSC planners.

Cross, Dr. Larry: Absonoja, Febe; and Garcia, Frannie. "Self-Survey:
Towards a New Approach to Conducting Surveys in the Develop-
ing World." Philippines: Philippine International Institute of Rural
Development, 1980. Also available as a condensed article from
Rural Reconstruction Review, 1981.

The study assesses the trade off of using voluntary community
participants instead of university trained research aides in conducting survey work.

Druben and Ricci Associates. "A Strategic (Self-) Evaluation", Vienna,
VA: Institute for International Development, Inc. 1980.

Excerpts from an in-depth evaluation of IIDI policies in a strategic
framework, which led to significant policy changes.

Evaluation Committee chaired by Cheigh, Hong-Sik. *Analysis and
Evaluation of Wonseong County Model Nutrition Education Project.* Davis, CA: MFM/FFH September 1980. (published report)

A comprehensive evaluation study conducted by Meals For
Millions/Freedom From Hunger Foundation in cooperation with
the local Korean county government. AID funded the study which
involved an exhaustive nutritional status survey on a random
sampling basis.

Foster Parents Plan International, *Plan's Planning and Evaluation
System.* Providence, RI: FPPI, 1981.

Includes FPPI's procedures for planning, *Situation Assessment
and General Establishment* — (SAGE), and evaluation, *Integrated
Evaluation and Research Process* (IERP). For our purposes, the
IERP is most relevant including six pages of reporting forms used
by field personnel.

Heifer Project International, *Evaluation Manual.* Little Rock, AR:
HPI, May 1982.

The culmination of four years work, HPI's manual is especially useful to anyone involved in livestock production projects. It contains general conceptual information about evaluation as well as specific tools suggested for field use.

The manual stemmed from a series of field tests. One example is "Evaluation Field Test IV: Philippine Rural Life Center Livestock Program", 1981. The report evaluates HPI's involvement in this project and makes specific recommendations to the boards of directors of the two organizations.

Hoskins, Marilyn W. and Weber, Fred R. "Evaluation of Lutheran World Relief Projects—Niger." New York: LWR, 1982. (duplicated report)

A comprehensive impact assessment of LWR's Niger program, including visits to thirteen sites where well-building projects were implemented in the wake of widespread drought that affected the country in 1975.

Kindervatter, Suzanne. "Striving for an Ideal: The OEF Participatory Evaluation System." (mimeographed) Washington: Overseas Education Fund, 1982.

This paper describes the methodology developed by the OEF during 1980-1982 period. It stresses a participatory approach and offers some practical lessons learned through experience.

Miller, Donald. "Project Tracking System". Wheaton, IL: MAP International, November 1980.

This paper outlines the tracking system currently used by MAP as a guide for field staff to plan and monitor project activity. It contains interesting information to help field staff identify community changes and 'to quantify' qualitative change noted through observation.

Overseas Education Fund, "Improvement of the Socio-Economic Conditions of Low-Income Women, Aged 25-50 through the Strengthening of the Union of Moroccan Women." 1982. (duplicated report)

A mid-point evaluation coordinated by an outside evaluator, this report describes an application of the OEF participatory evaluation approach. Details of the evaluation process, data gathered and recommendations comprise its contents.

Solidarios. "Numero Especial: La Evaluacion de Projectos de Desarrollo Social", *Solidarios*, No. 18, July-September 1981. (Spanish only)

Solidarios is the Council of American Development Foundations, and it publishes this magazine quarterly. This issue focuses on evaluation in Latin America, and stresses community participation in the process. It includes two articles: "Participative Evaluation of Social Development Projects" by Tito Quiros R. and "Self Evaluation of Development projects" by Fernando Osario Molinski. Write: Solidarios A.P. 620, Santo Domingo, Dominican Republic.

World Education, Inc. "Special Issue on Evaluation", *World Education Reports* updated reprint. September 1980. (Also in French and Spanish.)

An interesting collection of World Education experiences relating to field evaluation.

3. Priority Evaluation Texts:

Most evaluation texts are written by evaluation professionals, but PVO practitioners can profit from a selected review of the literature, particularly the latest thinking in the field. We recommend three recent texts for every PVO library:

Guba, Egon G. and Lincoln, Yvonna S. *Effective Evaluation: Improving the Usefulness of Evaluation Results through Responsive and Naturalistic Approaches*. San Francisco: Jossey-Bass Publishing, 1981.

Especially recommended to those interested in naturalistic evaluation and the qualitative methods associated with it. The authors build upon Robert Stake's responsive evaluation strategy and present a series of chapters devoted to the principle methods — interviewing, observation, analysis of documents and unobtrusive measures. The last part of the book details the actual process of an evaluation of this type and covers such items as initiating and organizing the evaluation, identifying key issues and concerns, gathering of information and reporting results. Of particular interest is a chapter on the "Evaluation as Instrument" which discusses its advantages and disadvantages, presents the qualities needed to be a good interviewer and observer, and suggests ways that such qualities can be improved in those willing to make the effort. Helpful thoughts for those concerned with training staff in qualitative techniques.

Patton, Michael Q. *Qualitative Evaluation Methods*. Beverly Hills, Calif: Sage Publications, 1980.

Highly recommended for anyone seriously interested in studying qualitative methods for evaluation. This well-written book discusses both conceptual issues and techniques for collecting and analyzing qualitative information. On the conceptual side, there is a full discussion of what qualitative data and methods are, and their compatibility with a series of evaluation models. On the more practical side, detailed guidance is offered on observation and qualitative interviewing, and on what to do with the reams of material collected by utilizing these two approaches. Examples are interspersed throughout, many coming from the author's own experience (Patton served as the Director of the Minnesota Center for Social Research and coordinated evaluations for many education and human service programs in the U.S. and overseas). The book is also enlivened by the insertion of quotes from "Halcolm," an evaluation sage invented by the author, whose laws, beatitudes, parables, chronicles, and proverbs wryly demonstrate major points about the joys and difficulties of doing an evaluation.

Rossi, Peter H. and Freeman, Howard E. *Evaluation: A Systematic Approach*, 2nd edition. Beverly Hills, Calif.: Sage Publications, 1982.

A sound, basic textbook in evaluation, which presents the classic, goal-based approach. It offers detailed explanations and examples of experimental and quasi-experimental design, succinct definitions of major concepts, and a full treatment of cost-benefit analysis. Most often used in university courses, the presentation of ideas is somewhat academic in nature, but it is certainly not beyond any PVO staffer interested in a comprehensive introduction to what has been the dominant approach in the field.

In addition to these recent texts, we also recommend two series which are breaking new ground in evaluation thinking. We found one publication from each series to be particularly helpful, but more are coming. The two are:

Smith, Nick L., editor. *Field Assessments of Innovative Evaluation Methods*. New Directions for Program Evaluation Series, Number 13. San Francisco: Jossey-Bass Publishing, 1982.

The series is a publication of the Evaluation Research Society. This book contains six articles discussing techniques that come from diverse disciplines: geography, law, journalism, art, anthropology and economics. The novelty of the book is the use of real-life cases where these techniques, all new to evaluation practice, are employed. Although this book does not provide easily transferable models, it should convince everyone that evaluation is no longer a narrowly confined field. Jossey-Bass Publishers, 433 California Street, San Francisco, CA 94104.

Smith, Nick L., editor. *New Techniques for Evaluation*. New Perspectives in Evaluation, vol. 2. Beverly Hills, Calif.: SAGE Publications, 1981.

The series is published in cooperation with the Northwest Regional Educational Laboratory. This volume supports the use of alternatives to the social science research methods that dominate evaluation. The five chapters cover a broad range of topics, from cost analysis to an exploratory view of how to evaluate evaluations. Particularly intriguing for PVO practitioners should be Egon Guba's chapter on investigative journalism and the application of its techniques in evaluation. SAGE Publications, Inc. 275 South Beverly Drive, Beverly Hills, CA 90212.

4. Background Evaluation Literature

Cook, Thomas D. and Reichardt, Charles S., editors. *Qualitative and Quantitative Methods in Evaluation Research*, Vol. 1. Sage Research Progress Series in Evaluation. Beverly Hills, Calif: Sage Publications, 1979.

This volume provides helpful insights into the quantitative - qualitative debate among evaluation researchers, and some of the efforts to achieve rapproachement between the methods. Of particular interest is the article by Reichardt and Cook, "Beyond Qualitative *versus* Quantitative Methods," which discusses the paradigms underlying the two approaches and suggests that methods are not necessarily linked to one or the other. In addition, the article by M.G. Trend, "On the Reconciliation of Qualitative and Quantitative Analysis: A Case Study," discusses an interesting case in which highly discrepant findings produced by participant observers on the one hand, and questionnaire surveys, on the other, were reconciled in a way that went well beyond the original reports in offering insight into the data. For those concerned with an anthropological approach to evaluation, Michael S. Knapp's article "Ethnographic Contributions to Evaluation Research: The Experimental Schools Program Evaluation and Some Alternatives," discusses the elements of ethnography applicable to evaluation projects.

Edwards, Ward; Guttentag, Marcia; and Snapper, Kent, "A Decision - Theoretic Approach to Evaluation Research" in E.L. Struening and M. Guttentag, editors. *Handbook of Evaluation Research*, Vol. 1. Beverly Hills, Calif: Sage Publications, 1975, pp 139-181.

Only recommended to those with a strong interest in decision theoretic models, and willing to wade through a statistically oriented discussion of the complex procedure known as multiattri-bute utility measurement. The technique is designed to aid deci-sionmakers weigh the various elements of a decision, and to reach a conclusion that takes them into account in accordance with their importance. While the idea has merit especially in situations where there are multiple decisionmakers and values, PVO practi-tioners would need to be especially creative in adopting it to fit the usual situations we face. Best for the strong-hearted.

Eisner, Elliot W. *The Educational Imagination: On the Design and Evaluation of School Programs.* New York: MacMillan Publishing Company, Inc., 1979.

Readers interested in Eisner's ideas regarding the application of the methods of criticism to evaluation should go directly to chapter 11 of this book for a full exposition. The chapter identifies and dis-cusses "some of the assumptions, principles, and procedures used in educational connoisseurship and educational criticism" as Dr. Eisner puts it. It addresses the issues of reliability, validity, and generalization, those of greatest·concern to more quantitatively oriented evaluations. While the approach was clearly designed for use in the American educational establishment, the PVO reader can easily draw parallels. The extended discussion is somewhat academic in tone, but certainly comprehensible. It may provide useful insights to those concerned with strengthening the perceptual and judgmental capabilities of staff as an adjunct to more formal data collection activities in evaluation.

House, Ernest R. "Assumptions Underlying Evaluation Models," Educational Researcher Vol. 7 no. 3, 1978, pp 4-12. Reprinted in *Ernest R. House, Evaluating with Validity.* Beverly Hills, Calif.: Sage Publications, 1980.

The article and book which subsequently incorporated it contain a typology of eight evaluation models which House believes encom-pass the range of approaches currently practiced by profes-sionals. The labels used do not match exactly those in the Source-book, and the extended list includes a couple of approaches less useful to PVO practitioners. But House's summary and critique of their features can expand one's understanding of options in evaluation in a helpful way. Chapters 2 and 11 are the pertinent ones. The balance of the book contains a more philosophic discus-sion of the standards of evaluation (linking them to the fundamen-tal values of truth, beauty, and justice) and is recommended only to those with a more specialized interest in the subject, and who are willing to read a more academic presentation of ideas.

Parlett, Malcolm and Hamilton, David. "Evaluation as Illumination: A New Approach to the Study of Innovatory Programs." In *Evaluation Studies Review Annual*, Vol. 1, edited by Gene V. Glass, pp. 140-157. Beverly Hills, Calif: Sage, 1976.

For those interested in naturalistic evaluation, this article offers a succinct and helpful introduction. It contrasts the agricultural-botany paradigm which underlies experimental design with the anthropological paradigm which underlies naturalistic or, what the authors call, "illuminative" evaluation. The methodologies associated with the latter approach are discussed along with the problems and potentials which this strategy has to offer. It is a straightforward, short, readable summary of the subject.

Rippey, Robert M., ed. *Studies in Transactional Education.* Berkeley, Calif.: McCutchan Publishing Corporation, 1973.

This book defines transactional evaluation, offers case studies of its use in various settings, mainly educational, as well as discusses the theoretical underpinnings of the approach. Of general interest is an article by Francis G. Caro, "Issues in the Evaluation of Social Programs" which reviews the literature with regard to such matters as methodology, program development and administration, organizational context, utilization, and the evaluator's role. Recommended to those who wish to explore this example of a more naturalistic, evaluative strategy.

Scriven, Michael. "Pros and Cons about Goal-Free Evaluation," with comments by Daniel L. Stufflebeam, Marvin Alkin, W. James Popham, and George F. Kneller. *Evaluation Comment*, 1972, vol. 3, no. 4. "Goal-Free Evaluation." *In School Evaluation: The Politics and Process*, edited by Ernest R. House, pp. 319-28. McCutchan Publishing Corportion, 1973.

_____. "Evaluation Bias and its Control." *In Evaluation Studies Review Annual*, vol 1, edited by Gene V. Glass, pp. 119-39. Calif.: Sage Publications 1976.

These three articles present Scriven's rationale for goal-free evaluation as well as operational considerations. The first, "Prose and Cons" is most noteworthy for not only providing an extended discussion of the approach and its merits, but also for juxtaposing Scriven's remarks with comments by other leading evaluators. The conclusions, as one might expect, are mixed, and offer insight into all the issues surrounding this interesting and unusual model. Scriven demonstrates that he can understand the consternation goal-free evaluation may cause project staff. "Goal-Free Evaluation" presents a mythical and humorous first encounter between an administrator and an evaluator intending to apply this approach. At the end of the discussion, The administrator has greater understanding, but much less sympathy for the concept, and his preoccupation well represents what voluntary agency and counterpart staff may feel if faced with a pure goal-free model. The last article discusses causes of evaluation bias and offers the goal-free approach as one method to overcome cetain factors related to this problem.

Stake, Robert E. *Evaluating the Arts in Education: A Responsive Approach.* Columbus, Ohio: Charles E. Merrill, 1975.

For those who want to learn more about responsive evaluation directly from the creator of this qualitatively-oriented approach, we recommend chapter 3. While the subject matter to which it was first applied is far from the usual for PVO development projects, the process Stake proposes can be readily adapted to our typical programs and relationships. The book is also eminently readable. CIRCE, a research and evaluation center which Stake heads, is most helpful in supplying reference material on his work. For more information, write to CIRCE: University of Illinois at Urban-Champaign, Room 270, 1310 South Sixth Street, Champaign, IL 61820.

Stufflebeam, Daniel et al. *Educational Evaluation and Decision-Making.* Itasca, Illinois: F.E. Peacock Publishers, Inc. 1971.

This book was written by the Phi Delta Kappa National Study Committee on Evaluation which included a number of notable evaluation professionals. It critiqued the field as it had evolved and proposed the CIPP (context-input-process-product) model of evaluation which utilized the decision as organizing focus for all evaluation activity. Detailed material is provided on the decision-making process and its relationship to evaluation as well as the CIPP model. Worksheets for tasks, methods and administration of an evaluation are also included. While written for the educational field, there is much of interest to PVO practitioners concerned with increasing utilization of evaluations by orienting them to the decision context.

Weiss, Carol H. *Evaluation Research: Methods of Assessing Program Effectiveness.* Englewood Cliffs, N.J.: Prentice-Hall, Inc. 1972.

The author describes this book as a basic text on evaluation research, written for undergraduate and graduate courses. "The basic theme of the book is that evaluation uses the methods and tools of social research but applies them in an action context that is intrinsically inhospitable to them." Within that frame-work,

Weiss deals with such subjects as evaluation purposes, for-
mulating program goals and developing appropriate measures to
assess, experimental, quasi- and non-experimental designs, program settings, and utilization. This is a helpful introduction to
traditional evaluation practice.

Weiss, Carol H. ed. *Evaluating Action Programs: Readings in Social
Action and Education*. Boston: Allyn and Bacon, Inc., 1972.

This collection contains some of the classics in the field including
Robert E. Stake's "The Countenance of Educational Evaluation,"
which presents a framework for looking at evaluation in a broader
context than just the measurement of outputs, and Michael
Scriven's "The Methodology of Evaluation," which first outlined
the distinction between formative and summative evaluation. Also
included are Alkin on decision-oriented evaluation, Carol Weiss
on utilization, Egon Guba on the failures of evaluation, and Campbell and Peter Rossi, among others, on experimental design. A
good introduction to the field of evaluation and the major figures in
the profession.

5. Colleague Agency and Other Source Material

ACTION. *Project Evaluation Handbook, Volume 1* and *Program Monitoring Handbook, Volume 2*, "Assessing Performance: A Reference
Series for the Field." Washington: ACTION, 1981.

These are the first two volumes of a series of four the Peace Corps
is producing for its staff and volunteers. They are detailed
reference books, but contain many ideas relevant to PVO practitioners. Volume 1 has more generally applicable material including sections on planning, implementation and/repor-
ting/utilization, each with various sample guides and worksheets.
Inquiries to: Frederick Williams, Peace Corps Evaluation Coordinator, ACTION, Washington, DC 25025.

Agency for International Development, Training and Development
Divisions. *Design and Evaluation of AID-Assisted Projects*.
Washington: AID, November 1980.

A comprehensive manual intended for the training of AID staff. It
covers the basic elements of AID's approach to evaluation including the logical framework, experimental design and statistical
analysis. Most of the presentation is clear enough for the non-
specialized practitioner to understand, even if not easily applicable to many PVO evaluation efforts. Inquiries to: Training and
Development Division, PM/TD/MA, AID Washington Training
Center, Washington, DC 20523.

Bennett, Claude. "Up the Heirarchy." *Journal of Extension*. March-
April 1975.

Dr. Bennett is an evaluation specialist for the U.S. Department of
Agriculture Extension Service. The article provides a heirarchy of
evidence acceptable for measuring impact that is relevant to our
current discussions. Includes examples of "hard and soft"
evidence.

Bruce, Robert L. "Programming for Intangibles", *Cornell Information
Bulletin #179*. September 1981.

The article explores the use of proxies for measuring intangible
objectives. Write: Distribution Center, 7 Research Park, Cornell
University, Ithaca, NY 14850.

Coombs, Philip H. ed. *New Strategies for Improving Rural Family Life*.
Essex, CT: International Council for Educational Development
1981.

A booklet which summarizes the findings of ICED's case studies of
innovative rural programs contained in the book Mr. Coombs
edited, *Meeting the Basic Needs of the Rural Poor*, ICED, 1980. It
briefly touches on the importance of evaluation. Its value is found
in the careful consideration of what makes rural programs succeed or fail. For this and other ICED publications, write: ICED
Publications, P.O. Box 217, Essex, CT 06426.

Elzinga, Aant "Evaluating the Evaluation Game: On the Methodology
of Project Evaluation, with Special Reference to Development
Cooperation," *SAREC Report*, 1981.

An introductory discussion of different evaluation methodologies,
it divides them into three paradigms: Neoclassical, "Dependencia"
and Self-Reliance. It mainly compares EEC, UN and World Bank
approaches but does raise some intriguing notions about evaluation that are revelant to PVOs. Inquiries to: Swedish Agency for
Research Cooperation with Developing Countries (SAREC) c/o
SIDA Birger Jarisgatan 61, S105 25 Stockholm, Sweden.

Hall, Bud; Etherington, Alan and Jackson, Ted. "Evaluation, Parti-
cipation and Community Health Care: Critique and Lessons."
Participatory Research Project, International Council for Adult
Education, November 1979 (reprint).

A critical look at standard evaluation approaches to health care
which may result in worsening the political situation of the poor.
The paper poses a participatory approach based on greater con-

trol and action by affected communities. For this and other ICAE publications, write: ICAE, 29 Prince Arthur Avenue, Toronto, Ontario, MSR 1B2 Canada.

Hatch, John. "A Record-Keeping System for Rural Households." Michigan State University Working Paper #9 (1980), 21 pp.

A description of novel techniques used to involve small farmers with little education in keeping records and a complete accounting of their farm activities. The paper is most relevant for those interested in participatory forms of data collection for evaluation purposes. It also includes illustrations of data sheets used by farmers. For a copy of this and other working papers, write: MSU Rural Development Working Papers, Department of Agricultural Economics, Michigan State University, East Lansing, MI 48823.

Johnson, Richard R. "Developing an Evaluation Policy." New York: Exxon Education Foundation, 1982 (mimeographed).

This paper was presented at a workshop for foundation personnel. Dr. Johnson also participated in our Wingspread conference on policy and evaluation. The paper outlines some different ways any granting agency can reflect on its role, which then influences evaluation policy.

Dr. Johnson has been a leader among foundation staff sharing a special interest in evaluation. With the support of the Council on Foundations and the Foundation Center, he has helped organize workshops to develop a foundation perspective on evaluation. We have found it beneficial to maintain an interchange with this effort. Any specific inquiries should be sent to Dr. Richard R. Johnson, Exxon Education Foundation, 47th floor, 111 West 49th St., New York, NY 10020.

Johnson, Richard R., ed. *Directory of Evaluation Consultants*. New York: The Foundation Center, 1981.

A comprehensive guide to organizations and individuals in the United States who do professional evaluations with indications of their past work and special areas of interest. Only a few may be known to PVOs, but it is useful to see the breadth and size of the "evaluation industry." Particularly useful is the Preface by Richard Johnson and Introduction by Michael Scriven, which discuss in practical terms how to decide on and deal with an evaluation consultant. Write: Foundation Center, 888 Seventh Avenue, New York, NY 10106.

Korten, David C. "Community Organization and Rural Development: A Learning Process Approach," Ford Foundation and Asian Institute of Management, *Public Administration Review*, September-October 1980.

An insightful study which looks at various successful Asian rural development efforts. Most useful is its contrast of "blueprint" to "learning process approach" to planning. It offers specific advice on how to implement a participatory approach to development. For single copies, write: Ford Foundation, Office of Reports, 320 East 43rd Street, New York, NY 10017.

Pyle, David F. "Framework for Evaluation of Health Sector Activities by Private Voluntary Organizations Receiving Matching Grants". Washington: Agency for International Development, 1982.

An AID-funded study that has had wide circulation among PVOs. Its purpose is "to serve as a frame of reference, providing common themes and some common standards which might be considered when reviewing PVO health-related activities." The paper presents interesting ideas for measuring qualitative process changes a community health program causes. Write: Judith Gilmore, Senior Evaluation Officer, Bureau for Food for Peace and Voluntary Assistance, United States International Development Cooperation Agency, AID, Washington, DC 20523.

Reading Rural Development Communications, *Bulletin 14*. Reading, England: University of Reading, April 1982.

The Rural Development Centre in Reading is well known for its practical, applied work in development. This issue of the *Bulletin* is devoted to evaluation, with articles on project appraisal and evaluation, the evaluation of social development and participatory evaluation. Case studies are drawn from OXFAM/England's experience. Most of the evaluation concepts in these articles have distinct parallels to the ideas covered in our workshops. Write: Agricultural Extension and Rural Development Centre, London Road, Reading, RG 1 5AQ England.

Steele, Sara M. "Qualitative and Quantitative Approaches in Program Evaluation," July 1981. (mimeographed).

Dr. Steele sent us this article after participating in the conference on evaluation and policy. The topic is directly relevent to PVO concerns about evaluation.

_____. *"Use of Evaluation in Resource* Management Decisions," February 1981. (mimeographed)

A paper presented to cooperative extensionists on ways to make evaluation more useful to decisions involving resource management.

_____. "Understanding and Working in Different Evaluation Worlds," January 1981. (mimeographed)

An intriguing paper intended for cooperative extension agents which addresses the question of how to balance the needs of different evaluation audiences. These three articles are only a sample of Dr. Steele's prolific writing on evaluation. Her work in the United States suggests many parallels with the evaluation concerns of PVOs working overseas. It provides a strong argument for encouraging more interchange with these type of applied programs in the U.S. universities. Write: Dr. Sara Steele, University of Wisconsin, Department of Vocational Education, 112 Teacher Education Building, 225 North Mills Street, Madison, WI 53706.

Soumelis, Constantin G. "Project Evaluation Methodologies and Techniques." Paris: UNESCO, 1977.

A handbook intended for UNESCO use, this treatment is one of the best for educational programs. Starting with a general vision of the function of evaluation, it suggests a framework for designing evaluation and examples of how to apply the framework. For this and other UN publications, write: UNIPUB, Box 433, Murray Hill Station, New York, NY 10016.

Suarez, Dr. Francisco, and Lic. Calatroni, Maria T. "Evaluacion de Programas de Accion Social". Buenos Aires: CIDES (Centro Interamericano Para El Desarrollo Social), undated. (mimeographed)

Emphasizes evaluation as a tool for social action. A general discussion of ideas an evaluator should keep in mind when designing an evaluation.

Tendler, Judith. "Turning Voluntary Organizations into Development Agencies: Questions for Evaluation," AID Program Evaluation Discussion Paper No. 12. Washington: Agency for International Development, 1982.

This volume is part of the AID Evaluation Publication Series, which includes program evaluations, project impact evaluations, special studies and discussion papers. This volume deals with the specific concerns of PVO evaluations. The author studied a sample of PVO evaluation reports as a means of raising a number of challenging questions about the assumptions behind PVO programs. For this volume and other AID evaluation publications, write: Editor of ARDA, S&T/AIU/DI Bureau for Science and Technology, AID, Washington, DC 20523.

Notes

Notes

Notes